Editor
Mary S. Jones, M.A.

Editor in Chief
Karen J. Goldfluss, M.S. Ed.

Cover Artist
Barb Lorseyedi

Imaging
James Edward Grace
Craig Gunnell

Publisher

Mary D. Smith, M.S. Ed.

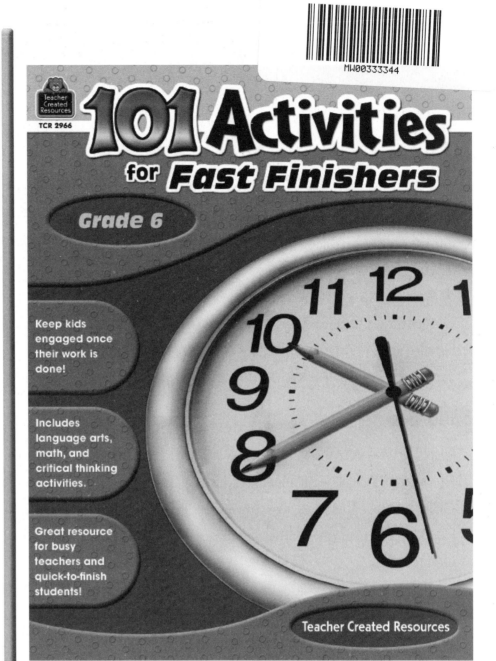

TCR 2966

101 Activities
for *Fast Finishers*

Grade 6

Keep kids engaged once their work is done!

Includes language arts, math, and critical thinking activities.

Great resource for busy teachers and quick-to-finish students!

Teacher Created Resources

Teacher Created Resources
6421 Industry Way
Westminster, CA 92683
www.teachercreated.com
ISBN: 978-1-4206-2966-8

©2011 Teacher Created Resources
Reprinted, 2012
Made in U.S.A.

Teacher Created Resources

Education Station
www.educationstation.ca
1-877-TEACH 'EM
1-877-832-2436

TABLE OF CONTENTS

INTRODUCTION

All students work at different speeds. Many take about the same amount of time to finish their work. Some are slower than others, and some are faster than others. You've probably been asked, "I'm done, what do I do now?" more times than you can count. But what's a teacher to do when one or more students finish early? The activity pages in *101 Activities for Fast Finishers* are the answer.

The 101 activities in this book focus on language arts, math, and critical thinking, and are divided as follows:

- Lively Language Arts (35 activities)
- Mind-Bender Math (35 activities)
- Beyond Brainy (31 activities)

Each activity has been labeled with an approximate amount of time that it will take students to complete. The estimated times range from 5 to 20 minutes. It is recommended that you copy, in advance, several pages representing the different times, and have them on hand to distribute, as needed. When a student asks you that famous "What do I do now?" question, a quick look at the clock will tell you which activity to give him or her. These activities will also be helpful to keep in your emergency substitute file as filler activities.

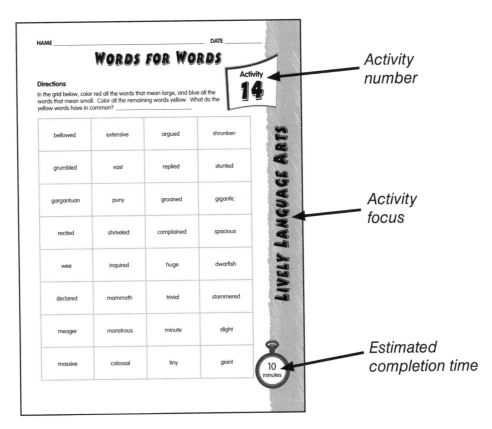

Activity number

Activity focus

Estimated completion time

WORD WEB

Activity 1

Directions

How many words can you find in the web below? Start at any letter and follow the threads to make your words.

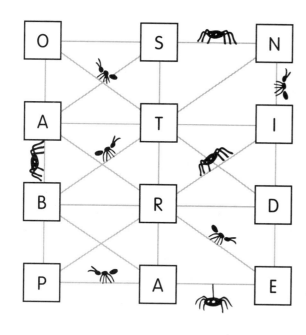

_____

_____

_____

_____

_____

_____

_____

_____

_____

_____

_____

_____

_____

LIVELY LANGUAGE ARTS

5 minutes

SCRAPBOOK

Activity 2

Directions

Using the letters in the word *scrapbook*, find the words to match the clues below. You may use a letter in any word only as often as it occurs in *scrapbook*.

S C R A P B O O K

1. chef: _____

2. you wear it on your foot: _____

3. sea creature: _____

4. tree that has acorns: _____

5. male pig: _____

6. hooded snake: _____

7. hard stone: _____

8. automobile: _____

9. grassy area to picnic in: _____

10. police officer: _____

11. thief: _____

12. type of fish: _____

10 minutes

SMALL WORDS

Activity 3

Directions

Find a small word inside the words in the box and place it correctly in each sentence. The first one has been done for you.

eleph<u>ant</u>	attention	water	related	spear
gorilla	plows	intestines	super	machinery

1. An _____ ant _____ is a hard working insect.

2. Mr. Smith has been _____ in the hospital for many weeks.

3. The teacher gave us a spelling _____ this morning.

4. The bully punched him on the _____.

5. I ate a juicy _____ for my lunch.

6. At the camp, I slept in a canvas _____.

7. We _____ dinner at 6:00 last night.

8. Morgan jumped easily over the _____ wall.

9. Mom said it's too _____ to have dessert.

10. The little boy was _____ to no good.

5 minutes

LIVELY LANGUAGE ARTS

WORD CHANGES

Activity **4**

Directions

In each box, make the top word into the bottom word by changing one letter at a time. Each step must make a real word.

1.

GIRL
MALE

3.

DIET
CARE

2.

SPIN
PLOT

4.

WALLS
TIGER

10 minutes

Lively Language Arts

SCRAMBLED WORDS

Activity 5

Directions

In five minutes, can you unscramble these common words? Ready, go!

1. ymept _____
2. lhwee _____
3. emsil _____
4. dofun _____
5. yadis _____
6. lacme _____
7. refve _____
8. yaprt _____
9. tahbi _____
10. mtsor _____

11. nabco _____
12. prgou _____
13. eohrs _____
14. dpsee _____
15. nimde _____
16. garny _____
17. mhotu _____
18. ewtir _____
19. tirna _____
20. ebetle _____

LIVELY LANGUAGE ARTS

5 minutes

DOUBLE LETTERS

Activity

6

Directions

Answer each clue with a word that contains double letters. The first one has been done for you.

1. A car is dependent on this. _____ wh**ee**ls _____

2. This crunchy candy tastes rich and buttery. _____

3. Filling in one of these indicates your answer. _____

4. This is where you might dance a waltz or tango. _____

5. This is a season for swimming pools and ice cream. _____

6. This is a group of people gathered to organize something. _____

7. You don't want this to fall off your clothes! _____

8. Use one of these when it rains. _____

9. You might feel this if you see a large spider! _____

10. What you do when you're against a decision. _____

11. You might send this to a faraway friend or relative. _____

12. This is what the dish ran away with in the nursery rhyme. _____

13. This vegetable is a key ingredient in coleslaw. _____

14. This is a seasoning, but don't use too much! _____

15. These are people between the ages of 13 and 19. _____

16. This word refers to that which is not first or last. _____

LIVELY LANGUAGE ARTS

10 minutes

SYLLABLES TO WORDS

Activity
1

Directions

Choose one syllable from column A, one from B, and one from C to form a three-syllable word. Write the new word in column D. Hint: One word in group 1 is the Spanish word for "party."

Column A	Column B	Column C	Column D
mi	cle	ance	_____
car	o	struct	_____
re	low	ta	_____
dis	cro	sphere	_____
hem	pen	mate	_____
es	es	us	_____
nu	i	lel	_____
al	con	ter	_____
par	ti	wave	_____
fi	al	bey	_____

won	a	dy	_____
im	e	el	_____
un	li	ry	_____
trag	fi	ful	_____
live	or	ous	_____
bound	der	ize	_____
gov	rav	cial	_____
spe	ern	sive	_____
vig	cial	hood	_____
of	pres	ment	_____

20
minutes

LIVELY LANGUAGE ARTS

HEADS OR TAILS

Activity

8

Directions

Each phrase below is a clue for an answer that contains either "head" or "tail."

1. an advantage at the start of a race   h e a d __ __ __ __ __

2. to drive dangerously close behind another vehicle   t a i l __ __ __ __

3. a descriptive title of a news story   h e a d __ __ __ __

4. one who makes clothes   t a i l __ __

5. a center of operations   h e a d __ __ __ __ __ __ __ __

6. the red rear light of a vehicle   t a i l __ __ __ __ __

7. having pain   h e a d __ __ __ __

8. the lowest or last part   t a i l __ __ __

9. progress   h e a d __ __ __

10. an aircraft's spiral dive   t a i l __ __ __ __

11. worn to keep back hair   h e a d __ __ __ __

12. an offensive position in football   t a i l __ __ __ __

13. deeply in love   h e a d __ __ __ __ __ __ __ __ __

14. the part of a car that discharges the exhaust of the engine   t a i l __ __ __ __

15. a bright light on the front of a car   h e a d __ __ __ __ __

LIVELY LANGUAGE ARTS

10 minutes

SYNONYMS

Activity 9

Directions

Fill in the crossword puzzle with the synonym of the words below. Use the words in the box to help you. Clue #8 Across has been done for you.

short	step
side	still
sight	stop
sign	strange
similar	sum
single	supply
small	suppose
solution	sure
space	system
spread	tall
spring	teacher
stand	tell
stay	

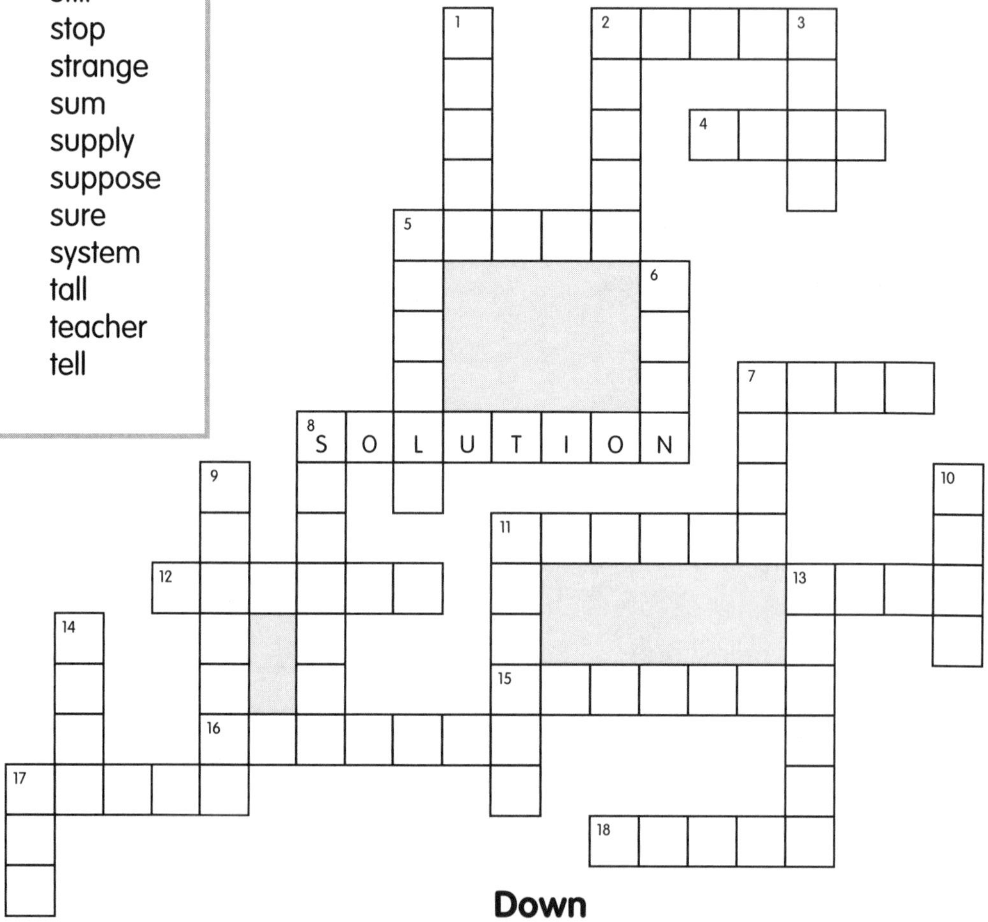

LIVELY LANGUAGE ARTS

(Crossword grid with 8 Across filled in: S O L U T I O N)

Across

2. brief, limited, scanty, deficient
4. high, lofty, towering, elevated
5. quiet, calm, stagnant, peaceful
7. margin, edge, behalf
8. explanation, answer, resolution
11. furnish, afford, provide, give
12. leap, bound, jump
13. certain, unmistakable, stable
15. explainer, illustrator, instructor
16. unfamiliar, unusual, odd
17. room, expanse, distance
18. rest, remain, stop, endure

Down

1. seeing, view, vision, spectacle
2. little, diminutive, insignificant
3. state, disclose, divulge, inform
5. one, only, individual, sole
6. indications, symptom, mark, signal
7. remain, continue, dwell
8. like, resembling, alike
9. presume, believe, think, guess
10. advance, pace, walk, action
11. method, classification, rule
13. extend, stretch, expand
14. suspend, obstruct, end
17. count, calculate, compute

15 minutes

ANTONYMS

Activity
10

Directions

In the word search, find an antonym for each of the words below.
Use the words in the box to help you.

```
R   E   P   A   S   T   P   L   U   R   A   L
A   R   P   O   F   R   A   S   H   D   A   A
P   T   R   S   H   N   R   E   J   E   C   T
Z   R   E   M   O   T   E   V   R   R   O   R
A   Y   T   I   P   P   F   T   A   I   R   U
P   D   T   Q   U   O   R   A   I   S   E   D
E   A   Y   R   O   Q   E   O   O   E   G   E
R   E   D   U   C   E   S   S   B   I   E   N
H   R   N   L   O   O   H   O   O   L   N   F
A   T   A   E   R   T   E   R   E   E   E   L
P   R   R   A   R   R   D   I   P   A   R   M
S   Q   U   E   S   T   I   O   N   S   G   A
```

past	questions	ready	remote
perhaps	quiet	real	retreat
plural	raised	reduce	rise
pretty	rapid	refreshed	rude
problem	rational	reject	rule

1. solution
2. irrational
3. fall
4. sluggish
5. fake
6. singular
7. exception

8. respectful
9. exhausted
10. lowered
11. future
12. ugly
13. definitely
14. loud

15. near
16. advance
17. unprepared
18. increase
19. accept
20. answers

15 minutes

STRIKE OUT

Activity 11

Directions

Color the word in each row that **cannot** be made from the letters in the word in capitals that begins the row. Each letter can be used only once.

1.	ARITHMETIC	cream	heart	heard	mate	came
2.	FORTNIGHT	tonight	naught	tight	fright	thing
3.	CREATURE	create	tear	trace	curate	center
4.	PARADISE	draper	praise	spire	parade	spider
5.	CONSISTENTLY	silent	costly	sister	scones	scent
6.	MOUNTAINS	stain	mouse	mint	satin	atoms
7.	INCREDIBLE	bridle	rind	blind	dribble	binder
8.	ENVIRONMENT	vine	more	torn	entire	money
9.	ANYTHING	hint	thin	gain	hinge	gnat
10.	TASTEFUL	latter	steal	fuel	slate	leaf
11.	ADORABLE	bear	drab	bleed	real	road
12.	FURNITURE	true	nurture	fire	return	nature

LIVELY LANGUAGE ARTS

10 minutes

CONNECTIONS

Activity 12

Directions

Think of a word that could be used with each term to make a compound word or a phrase. The word can go before or after the given words.

Example: foot	game	snow	___ball___
1. opera	box	hand	_____
2. head	Easter	fried	_____
3. line	flies	down	_____
4. whipped	sour	cheese	_____
5. shelter	atomic	time	_____
6. book	garbage	pipe	_____
7. light	cards	back	_____
8. go	wheel	shopping	_____
9. moon	night	year	_____
10. city	way	mark	_____
11. Adam's	tree	core	_____
12. ballpoint	pal	pig	_____
13. power	shoe	race	_____
14. birds	sick	puppy	_____
15. ball	lid	pink	_____

LIVELY LANGUAGE ARTS

10 minutes

ORIGINS

Activity
13

Directions

Use a dictionary that gives word origins to find out where these words came from and what they mean.

1. toucan — _____

_____

2. chocolate — _____

_____

3. gazette — _____

_____

4. spaghetti — _____

_____

5. yacht — _____

_____

6. curry — _____

_____

7. dandelion — _____

_____

8. anthology — _____

_____

LIVELY LANGUAGE ARTS

10
minutes

WORDS FOR WORDS

Directions

In the grid below, color red all the words that mean large, and blue all the words that mean small. Color all the remaining words yellow. What do the yellow words have in common? _____

bellowed	extensive	argued	shrunken
grumbled	vast	replied	stunted
gargantuan	puny	groaned	gigantic
recited	shriveled	complained	spacious
wee	inquired	huge	dwarfish
declared	mammoth	trivial	stammered
meager	monstrous	minute	slight
massive	colossal	tiny	giant

LIVELY LANGUAGE ARTS

10 minutes

17

FILL-UPS

In 15 minutes, how many words can you make by filling in the letter blanks below? Try to make at least 20.

Activity 15

_____ _____ _____ S T

_____ _____ _____

_____ _____ _____

_____ _____ _____

_____ _____ _____

_____ _____ _____

_____ _____ _____

_____ _____ _____

_____ _____ _____

_____ _____ _____

15 minutes

LIVELY LANGUAGE ARTS

WHICH WORD?

Directions

Words that sound alike or look alike often have meanings that are not alike. Decide which word is the correct one, and then color in that box.

1.	to leave out	accept	except
2.	the result	effect	affect
3.	a building	capital	capitol
4.	to give advice	consul	counsel
5.	to hint at or suggest	imply	infer
6.	second of two things	later	latter
7.	previously	all ready	already
8.	immovable	stationary	stationery
9.	in front of	proceed	precede
10.	the beginning of life	birth	berth
11.	state of the atmosphere	whether	weather
12.	occurring yearly	annual	perennial
13.	temperament	disposition	deposition
14.	lesson	morale	moral
15.	a small island	aisle	isle

LIVELY LANGUAGE ARTS

10
minutes

SHRINKING WORDS

Directions

Drop one letter at a time to make another word. Each time you take away a letter it must spell a real word.

Example: gasps ➔ gaps ➔ gas ➔ as ➔ a

1. STARTLING

➔ _____
➔ _____
➔ _____
➔ _____
➔ _____
➔ _____
➔ _____

3. CREMATED

➔ _____
➔ _____
➔ _____
➔ _____
➔ _____
➔ _____

2. CHEATED

➔ _____
➔ _____
➔ _____
➔ _____
➔ _____
➔ _____

4. SPRINTS

➔ _____
➔ _____
➔ _____
➔ _____
➔ _____

5
minutes

Roman Numeral Code

Activity 18

Directions

Use the Roman numeral code to discover a list of difficult words to spell. Write each letter beneath the Roman numeral that stands for it. An example has been done for you.

I = a	II = b	III = c	IV = d	V = e	VI = f	VII = g	VIII = h	IX = i
X = j	XI = k	XII = l	XIII = m	XIV = n	XV = o	XVI = p	XVII = q	XVIII = r
XIX = s	XX = t	XXI = u	XXII = v	XXIII = w	XXIV = x	XXV = y	XXVI = z	

Example:

XIX	XV	XII	IV	IX	V	XVIII
s	o	l	d	i	e	r

1. XII IX III V XIV XIX V

2. VI I XIII IX XII IX I XVIII

3. I   XII XV XX

4. III I XII V XIV IV I XVIII

5. XXII I III XXI XXI XIII

6. XXIII V IX XVIII IV

7. VI XV XVIII V IX VII XIV

8. XVIII VIII XXV XX VIII XIII

9. V XIII II I XVIII XVIII I XIX XIX

10. I XVI XVI XVIII XV XVI XVIII IX I XX V

11. I III III XV XIII XIII XV IV I XX V

12. XVI XVIII IX XXII IX XII V VII V

13. VII XXI I XVIII I XIV XX V V

14. IX XVIII XVIII V XII V XXII I XIV XX

15. XIX V XVI I XVIII I XX V

LIVELY LANGUAGE ARTS

10 minutes

FUNNY HELPING VERBS

Activity 19

Directions

Write the helping verb(s) to complete each joke. The most common helping verbs are in the box. Some are used more than once.

am	was	has	have	would	did	could
are	were	had	will	do	can	

1. Why did George Washington stand in the boat as he crossed the Delaware River?

   . . . If he _____ sat down, they _____ _____ given him an oar.

2. Why _____ the employee fall asleep at work?

   . . . Her boss told her she _____ retire early.

3. What did the employment agent say to the unemployed vegetable?

   . . . "Don't worry. I _____ sure something _____ turnip soon."

4. Why did the light turn red?

   . . . So would you, if you _____ caught changing in the middle of the street!

5. Why did the bear tiptoe through the campground?

   . . . He _____ not want to wake up the sleeping bags.

6. What's the world's quietest game?

   . . . Bowling, because you _____ hear a pin drop.

7. Why did the farmer use a steamroller on his potato field?

   . . . He _____ raising mashed potatoes.

8. Judge: "The jury _____ found you innocent of stealing jewelry."

   Defendant: "Does that mean I _____ keep it?"

9. Girl: "Why _____ you keep a stick of dynamite in your car's glove compartment?"

   Boy: "To fix flat tires without using the jack."

   Girl: "What _____ you talking about?"

   Boy: "If I get a flat tire, I _____ just blow it up."

10. Why couldn't anyone find the deck of cards?

    . . . They _____ been lost in the shuffle.

10 minutes

LIVELY LANGUAGE ARTS

PREPOSITIONS

Activity
20

Directions

Some of the most common prepositions are listed in the box. Circle the prepositions in the first group of sentences. Then add prepositions to complete the second group of sentences.

1. My grandparents performed in the circus.

2. Grandpa used to walk on the tightwire.

3. Beneath him, the audience gasped.

4. Grandma stood on the back of a horse.

5. It galloped around the ring, but she never fell.

6. During the performance, people sold popcorn.

7. Kids crowded across benches, talking and laughing.

8. Between acts, my grandparents mended costumes.

9. They kept extra fabric inside a trailer.

10. They ate dinner outside with the other performers.

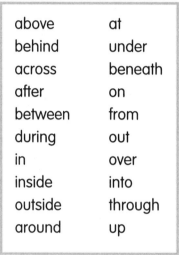

above	at
behind	under
across	beneath
after	on
between	from
during	out
in	over
inside	into
outside	through
around	up

11. The treasure is buried _____ a bridge.

12. First, you have to walk ten paces _____ a field.

13. Then you have to crawl _____ a barbed wire fence.

14. Turn right, and walk _____ a hill.

15. _____ this point, you'll see a crooked tree.

16. Climb _____ it and look to your left.

17. You'll see the bridge _____ the tree.

18. Dig a hole _____ the big green boulder.

19. You'll see a box _____ a few minutes.

20. There, _____ the box, is the treasure!

15
minutes

LIVELY LANGUAGE ARTS

HOMOPHONES

Activity 21

Directions

Select the correct homophone from the parentheses to fill in the blanks in the sentences below.

1. Mrs. Ridley gave her _____ for all of us to watch the _____ of the colorful hot-air balloons as they rose over Albuquerque. *(ascent/assent)*

2. The sailors on the *Merry Mermaid* were trying to plot a safe _____ *(coarse/course)* through the _____. *(straight/strait)*

3. The furniture refinisher did not want to use the _____ sandpaper. *(coarse/course)*

4. Just as important as remembering to give a _____ to someone else is having the ability to accept one gracefully. *(compliment/ complement)*

5. Did you remember to _____ the references you used to write your report? *(cite/site)*

6. The climber kept the rope _____ as he made his way to the peak. *(taught/taut)*

7. If you look over _____ , you will see _____ house that they have painted red, white, and blue. *(their/there)*

8. Learning your _____ will _____ *(lessen/lesson)* the chance that you will earn a poor grade.

9. Your _____ is required while I open my _____. *(presence/presents)*

10. Lucinda _____ the test, and that got her _____ the one thing that she had been dreading the most. *(passed/past)*

10 minutes

FIRST AND LAST

Activity 22

Directions

Each of the following clues has an answer in which the first letter is the same as the last letter.

1. an official list of names   r _ _ _ _ r

2. an amount over and above what is needed   s _ _ _ _ _ s

3. a great work of art or literature   c _ _ _ _ _ c

4. a summary   s _ _ _ _ _ _ s

5. loss of memory   a _ _ _ _ _ a

6. a state   A _ _ _ _ _ a

7. a brief advertisement   b _ _ _ b

8. activity requiring physical exertion   e _ _ _ _ _ _ e

9. handwriting skill   p _ _ _ _ _ _ _ _ p

10. a word used by magicians   a _ _ _ _ _ _ _ _ _ _ a

11. to rub out   e _ _ _ e

12. a continent   A _ _ _ _ _ _ _ a

13. a bird   e _ _ _ e

14. showing great skill at doing something   t _ _ _ _ t

15. having made twice as much   d _ _ _ _ _ d

16. to strike a door with a fist   k _ _ _ k

17. to be born from an egg   h _ _ _ h

18. the act or words of welcoming someone   g _ _ _ _ _ _ g

19. one thousand years   m _ _ _ _ _ _ _ m

20. to regain health after illness   r _ _ _ _ _ r

15 minutes

WORD LADDERS

Directions

Transform one word into another by changing a single letter in each step so that each step in the ladder is a valid word. Use the hints at the right to help you.

1. Turn clap into away.

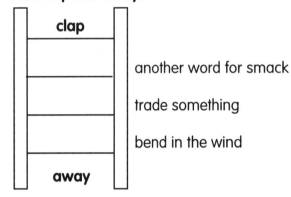

clap

another word for smack

trade something

bend in the wind

away

4. Turn game into ball.

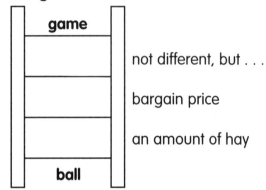

game

not different, but . . .

bargain price

an amount of hay

ball

2. Turn ink into pen.

ink

place to stay for the night

an electrically-charged atom

measure of weight

between nine and eleven

pen

5. Turn hand into foot.

hand

group of musicians

glue together

loving and affectionate

nourishment

foot

3. Turn ring into hand.

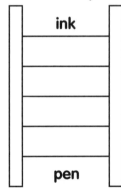

ring

the peel of an orange

to fasten together

group that plays instruments

hand

6. Turn malt into pies.

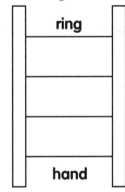

malt

not female

lacking in color

window glass

type of tree

puts the tail on the donkey

pies

15
minutes

LIVELY LANGUAGE ARTS

MEET ELIZABETH

Directions

This is Elizabeth. She wants to know how many different words you can make using the letters in her full name. The letters must be in the same order as in her name, for example, *hard*.

E L I Z A B E T H   C H A R R I E D

LIVELY LANGUAGE ARTS

_____   _____

_____   _____

_____   _____

_____   _____

_____   _____   _____

_____   _____   _____

_____   _____   _____

_____   _____

10 minutes

DICTIONARY DAZE

Activity
25

Directions

Use your dictionary to answer these questions. Give the first meaning of each word in your answer.

1. What is the longest word beginning with *ex*?

_____

_____

2. What word directly follows *lollipop*?

_____

_____

3. What word comes directly before *rhinoceros*?

_____

_____

4. What is the very last word in your dictionary?

_____

_____

5. What is the fifth word that starts with *in*?

_____

LIVELY LANGUAGE ARTS

10
minutes

ABBREVIATED WORDS

Directions

Underline the word in each sentence that is usually abbreviated.
Write the abbreviated form on the line.

LIVELY LANGUAGE ARTS

Example: I will send you a _facsimile_ of the contract.   _____ fax _____

1. Jesse's favorite disport is dodgeball.   _____

2. My favorite subject is mathematics.   _____

3. We drove our caravan to the national park.   _____

4. Maxine wore a new pair of pantaloons to school.   _____

5. Theo is such a baseball fanatic!   _____

6. I wish that autobus would be on time for once!   _____

7. Justin is taking pianoforte lessons from Mrs. Gregson.   _____

8. There was an advertisement in the newspaper.   _____

9. Have you ever been to the zoological gardens?   _____

10. Doctors forecast many cases of influenza this winter.   _____

11. Our physics teacher gave us an examination today.   _____

12. "Hand me the microphone," said Vivian.   _____

13. Violet will meet Wilma at three of the clock.   _____

14. We went to see _Batman_ at the local cinematograph.   _____

15. The coach said to meet in the gymnasium for practice.   _____

16. For Halloween, I disguised my hair under a periwig.   _____

10 minutes

FIGURATIVE LANGUAGE

Activity
27

LIVELY LANGUAGE ARTS

Directions

Create both a simile and a metaphor to describe each of the following events.

Example: a hummingbird feeding

Simile: Our resident hummingbird looks like a helicopter at the feeder.

Metaphor: Our resident hummingbird is a helicopter at the feeder.

1. a cat stalking a bird

Simile: _____

Metaphor: _____

2. a cowboy roping a calf

Simile: _____

Metaphor: _____

3. an alligator eating a fish

Simile: _____

Metaphor: _____

4. a student writing a paragraph

Simile: _____

Metaphor: _____

5. a girl skipping rope

Simile: _____

Metaphor: _____

6. a parent feeding a baby in a highchair

Simile: _____

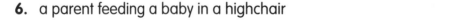

Metaphor: _____

20 minutes

GROWING SENTENCES

Directions

In ten minutes, write as many sentences as you can in which:

- the first word has only one letter
- the second has two letters
- the third has three letters . . . and so on.

Example: I am the last named father!

1. _____

2. _____

3. _____

4. _____

5. _____

6. _____

7. _____

8. _____

9. _____

10. _____

11. _____

12. _____

LIVELY LANGUAGE ARTS

10 minutes

ALPHABETICAL ORDER

Activity
29

Directions

All of the words in the box below begin the same. Some share the same ending letter. Write the words on the appropriate lines, and then rewrite them in alphabetical order.

comments	committee	command	complex	comparison
combined	communication	companion	computer	communicate
compass	complete	complicated	compare	company

1. Write the word that ends in *y*. _____

2. Write the word that ends in *x*. _____

3. Write the word that ends in *r*. _____

4. Write the two words that end in *s*. _____

5. Write the three words that end in *n*. _____

6. Write the three words that end in *d*. _____

7. Write the four words that end in *e*. _____

Alphabetical Order

a. _____ i. _____

b. _____ j. _____

c. _____ k. _____

d. _____ l. _____

e. _____ m. _____

f. _____ n. _____

g. _____ o. _____

h. _____

20
minutes

LIVELY LANGUAGE ARTS

VERB FORMS

Activity 30

Directions

Color the box that has the correct verb form from the choices given.

1. I should have [knew | known] that I could have [froze | frozen] my toes.

2. As soon as Manuel had [chose | chosen] his subject, he [began | begun] his talk.

3. The coat that I had [wore | worn] only once had been [stole | stolen] .

4. The dress that I would have [chose | chosen] was [tore | torn] .

5. Has the bell [rang | rung] , or would I [have | of] heard it here?

6. The man who had [stole | stolen] the money was [knew | known] by the police.

7. You should [have | of] known that the song was [sang | sung] by Marilyn.

8. Has he always [drove | driven] so carelessly, or has he just [began | begun] to do so?

9. She [began | begun] to see that she had [chose | chosen] the wrong topic.

10. Snow [fell | fallen] after the pond had [froze | frozen] .

11. Our doorbell is [wore | worn] out because the children have [rang | rung] it too many times.

12. Two cups have [fell | fallen] off the shelf and have [broke | broken] .

13. Barbara [sang | sung] the song that was [chose | chosen] by the committee.

14. I would have [brung | brought] my stereo if it hadn't been [stole | stolen] .

15. The telephone [rang | rung] just as I [began | begun] to study.

10 minutes

LIVELY LANGUAGE ARTS

PORTMANTEAU WORDS

Directions

A portmanteau word is a kind of abbreviated word where two or more words are put together to create an entirely new word. For example, *cheese* + *hamburger* = *cheeseburger*. Write the portmanteau words for the combinations below.

1. breakfast + lunch = _____

2. spoon + fork = _____

3. motor + pedal = _____

4. parachute + troops = _____

5. smoke + fog = _____

6. television + marathon = _____

7. twist + whirl = _____

8. travel + monologue = _____

9. gleam + shimmer = _____

10. motor + hotel = _____

11. motorcycle + cross country = _____

12. splash + spatter = _____

13. international + network = _____

14. flame + glare = _____

15. flutter + hurry = _____

16. clap + crash = _____

17. slop + slush = _____

18. electronic + mail = _____

19. camera + recorder = _____

20. hazardous + material = _____

LIVELY LANGUAGE ARTS

10 minutes

DENTIST'S TIPS

Activity
32

Directions

Read the following dental-health tips from your dentist. Use the mini dictionary to help you fill in the missing words. Then in the box below, match the ideas on the left to the words on the right.

---

pertinent — related to the point   **fester** — to decay
goad — to push into action   **quibble** — to oppose an idea
culprit — the thing that caused the trouble   **gargantuan** — huge

---

"It's good to see you for your regular checkup. Please relax now and sit back. Oh, dear, how can this be? I am finding a (**1.**) _____ cavity! What have you been eating since I saw you last, or haven't you been brushing?

"Listen to me carefully now. This information is very (**2.**) _____ . You need to brush often and avoid a lot of sweets. Otherwise, you'll have another tooth begin to (**3.**) _____ . I know I've told you these things before, but again I have to (**4.**) _____ you. You only have one set of teeth, and you need to keep them healthy! Watch what you eat and drink. Sugar is the real (**5.**) _____ . Please, remember, the next time your parents tell you that you are drinking too many soft drinks, don't (**6.**) _____ with them!"

---

7. a mouse that ate a hole in my sock	**A.** quibble
8. to disagree and speak against	**B.** pertinent
9. to strongly encourage	**C.** culprit
10. the size of the Grand Canyon	**D.** fester
11. to become an unhealthy condition	**E.** gargantuan
12. necessary to know	**F.** goad

10
minutes

Lively Language Arts

MASKING THE ODOR

Activity
33

Directions

Read the story, and then answer the questions that follow.

There once was a farmer who had over a hundred cows. He milked them each day and set them out into the pasture at night. His neighbor, a banker, had just moved in next door. The banker wanted to move to the country to enjoy the views.

On the first night, the banker sat outside to enjoy the sunset. He could scarcely breathe. The stench from the cows was so great. Disgusted, he went indoors. The next evening, he tried to enjoy the sunset again but was forced to go back inside because of the smell.

He finally decided that the farmer would have to go. The banker had a lot of money, so he offered to buy the farm.

"Yes, I will sell you the farm, but it will take me at least a week to sell the cows and take care of them. Would you be willing to wait a week?" asked the farmer.

The banker decided he could do that. At the end of the week, the banker approached the farmer again. The farmer wondered if they could wait until his visiting brother left. The banker consented. A month passed. The farmer approached the banker hesitantly to see if he still wanted the farm.

"Why, no," replied the banker. "You keep it."

The farmer smiled to himself. He knew that by making the banker wait, it would allow time for the banker to get used to the awful smell of the cows.

1. Which paragraph states the conflict in this story?
   a. second paragraph
   b. first paragraph
   c. third paragraph
   d. fifth paragraph

2. What is the conflict or problem of this story?
   a. The farmer doesn't know how to keep away the smell.
   b. The farmer is worried about offending the banker.
   c. The farmer's cows are extra smelly.
   d. The banker is unhappy with the smell of the cows.

3. What is the meaning of the word *hesitantly* as used in the passage?
   a. dejectedly   c. decidedly
   b. offensively   d. cautiously

10 minutes

LIVELY LANGUAGE ARTS

THE EYE

Activity 34

Directions

Read the passage, and then answer the questions that follow.

Have you ever wondered how the eye works? The human eye is about as big as a ping pong ball. It sits in the eye socket inside the skull. The eyelid protects the front part of the eye. The eyelid is a piece of skin that is movable so that it can open and close. The eyelid also helps keep the eye moist. It does this by blinking. Blinking is a voluntary and involuntary action. The eye blinks involuntarily several times a minute.

The eyelid also has great reflexes. This is a form of protection for the eye. If a ball or other object is coming towards the eye, the eyelid will quickly close to protect the eye. The eyelid will also close or squint when there is bright sunlight. The eyelashes are another important protection for the eye. Eyelashes keep dirt and other particles from getting into the eyes.

The white part of the eyeball is called the *sclera*. The sclera is the outside coating of the eyeball. Tiny blood vessels line the sclera. The cornea rests directly on top of the colored part of the eye. The cornea is completely transparent so that light can filter through. Behind the cornea are the iris and the pupil. The iris is the colorful part of the eye. The pupil determines how much light is allowed into the eye. The eye is an amazing part of the body.

LIVELY LANGUAGE ARTS

1. What is the purpose of the eyelashes?

    a. to keep the eye moist

    b. to allow light to filter into the eye

    c. to allow movement in the eye

    d. to keep dirt and other particles out of the eye

2. What part of the eye is the colorful part?

    a. cornea   c. iris

    b. pupil   d. sclera

3. Which paragraph helps you answer the previous question?

    a. third paragraph

    b. first paragraph

    c. second paragraph

    d. none of the above

10 minutes

PARAGRAPH PARTS

Activity
35

Directions

Read the paragraph, and then answer the questions that follow.

A Sunday Picnic in the Redwoods

(1) Because it was such a welcoming spring morning with the sun shining brightly on the golden California poppies, we decided to go on a Sunday picnic. (2) We packed a lunch of bananas and crunchy Fuji apples, sharp cheddar cheese and wheat crackers, and sweet peanut butter cookies. (3) Then, we began our one-mile hike to Jedediah Smith State Park. (4) As we turned toward the park picnic area, we noticed the pink and white flowers at the feet of the soaring redwood trees. (5) Those blooming trilliums were a colorful carpet on the floor of the forest. (6) When we reached the bank of the Smith River, we emerged into the sunshine again. (7) Before us was a small, sandy beach. (8) As we drew closer, we saw a father playing with his three young children at the edge of the river. (9) The water was clear and as green as sparkling emeralds. (10) However, even though the sunshine was warm, the water was as cold as ice. (11) The children would stick their toes into the water and then run, laughing, back to the warmth of the sand. (12) By the time we finished our lunch at one of the picnic tables beside the river, the children and father were packing up their beach toys and towels and getting into their car to leave. (13) All of us had enjoyed the sunny spring day. (14) We really liked the cheese.

---

1. Which sentence contains a simile?

   a. 1   b. 3   c. 8   d. 9

2. Which sentence contains a metaphor?

   a. 2   b. 5   c. 6   d. 9

3. Which of the following words in sentence 10 is used as a transition?

   a. even   b. However   c. was   d. cold

4. Which of the following sentences should be omitted from the paragraph?

   a. 2   b. 3   c. 11   d. 14

5. Which of the following sentences begins with a transition?

   a. 2   b. 3   c. 9   d. 11

15
minutes

BULL'S EYE

Activity

36

Directions

What are the ways to score exactly 100 on this dartboard with the number of darts as listed below?

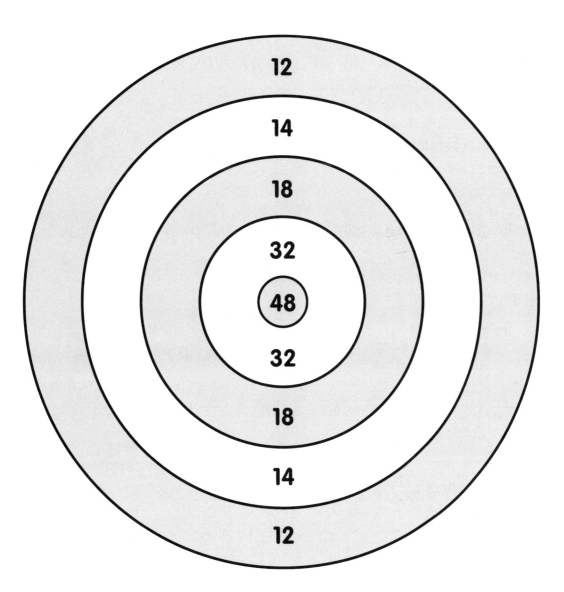

1. with 4 darts: _____

2. with 5 darts: _____

3. with 6 darts: _____

15 minutes

NUMBER FACTS

Activity 37

Directions

Use the row of numbers to answer the questions that follow.

| 11 | 12 | 13 | 14 | 15 | 16 | 17 | 18 | 19 | 20 | 21 | 22 | 23 |

1. What is the fifth odd number reading from left to right?   _____

2. What is the number exactly halfway between 17 and 23?   _____

3. What is the total of the first three even numbers reading from left to right?   _____

4. Add together every third number from left to right.   _____

5. What is the difference between the first number and the last number?   _____

6. What is the total of all the prime numbers?   _____

5 minutes

MIND-BENDER MATH

ADDITION BOX

Activity
3 8

Directions

Add across and down. If you are correct, your totals will match exactly (i.e., totals across and down) when added.

	E.		F.		G.		H.		
A.	379	+	743	+	538	+	653	=	_____
	+		+		+		+		+
B.	468	+	106	+	107	+	244	=	_____
	+		+		+		+		+
C.	372	+	293	+	300	+	117	=	_____
	+		+		+		+		+
D.	150		174		425		209	=	_____
	=		=		=		=		=
	_____	+	_____	+	_____	+	_____	=	[ ]

MIND-BENDER MATH

10 minutes

CLOCKS GALORE

Directions

Look at each clock face on the left. On the blank clock face at the right, draw the time that is indicated.

1.  3 1/4 hours later

2.  3 1/4 hours earlier

3.  6 hours 10 minutes earlier

4.  5 1/4 hours later

5.  3 hours 42 minutes later

6.  7 1/4 hours earlier

MIND-BENDER MATH

5 minutes

IDENTIFYING SHAPES

Activity
40

Directions

Using the clues below, draw and name each solid in the space at the right.

1. I have one rectangular face and my other faces are triangles. I also have five corners.

2. I have three rectangular faces and two equilateral triangular faces.

3. I have six vertices and ten edges. One of my faces is a regular pentagon.

4. I have eight faces and twelve vertices. Two of my faces are hexagons.

5. I have two names. I am made of four congruent shapes and have four vertices.

STOP AND THINK

Activity
41

Directions

Answer each math question below.

---

1. Traffic lights are arranged with red on top, yellow in the middle, and green at the bottom. How many other ways could these three colors be arranged? List them.

---

2. When you write the numbers 1 to 100, how many times is the digit 9 used?

3. What do these five numbers have in common?

9	4	25	36	16

10 minutes

MIND-BENDER MATH

SIMILAR AND CONGRUENT

Activity
42

Directions

Determine which of the shapes in each row are similar and which are congruent. Circle the similar shapes. Color the congruent shapes.

1.

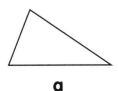 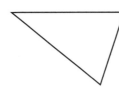 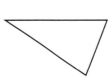

a   b   c   d

2.

a   b   c   d

3.

a   b   c   d

4.

a   b   c   d

5.

a   b   c   d

6.

a   b   c   d

MIND-BENDER MATH

10 minutes

BIG MONEY

Activity 43

Directions

Have you ever heard of the $5,000-bill? To discover whose picture is on it, find the difference in each problem below. Decode the name by matching the answer to its letter. Write the letter in the box below the difference.

1.	2.	3.	4.	5.
9,371	3,313	7,500	6,000	6,230
− 4,528	− 1,834	− 2,627	− 3,444	− 4,985

6.	7.	8.	9.	10.	11.	12.
7,927	7,203	5,361	7,455	4,079	8,752	5,386
− 3,054	− 5,724	− 3,142	− 3,679	− 2,834	− 6,273	− 2,174

1,479 **A**	3,776 **I**	4,843 **J**
2,219 **D**	4,873 **M**	2,556 **E**
3,212 **N**	1,245 **S**	2,479 **O**

15 minutes

WHAT NUMBER?

Activity 44

Directions

Can you figure out what each number is? Circle your final answer.

1. I am a number between 5 and 15. The sum of my digits is odd.
   One of the digits is twice the other.

2. I am a number between 20 and 50. One digit is half the other.
   The product of the digits is twice the sum of the digits.

3. I am a number over 200 but less than 300. All my digits are even.
   No two digits are the same. The sum of my digits is 12.

4. I am more than 100 but less than 200. I am divisible by 5. The sum
   and product of my digits are divisible by 5. My three digits are odd.

5. I am less than 50 but more than 20. The sum and product of my
   two digits are the same.

10 minutes

NUMBER DIAMONDS

Activity
45

Directions

Place a number from 1 to 8 in the circles so that each diamond adds up to 18. You can use each number only once.

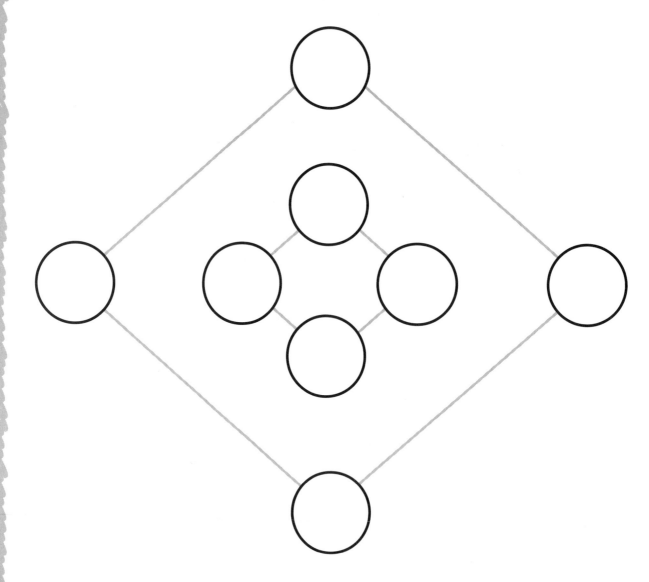

5
minutes

NUMBER WORDS

Activity **46**

Directions

How well do you know the numbers represented by words? Fill in the blank for each sentence below.

1. A period of ten years is a _____.

2. A stand with three legs is a _____.

3. A creature with one hundred legs is a _____.

4. A hexagon has _____ sides.

5. A sea creature with eight tentacles is an _____.

6. A song for two people is a _____.

7. Two things the same (e.g., socks) is a _____.

8. A vehicle with three wheels is a _____.

9. A quintet is a group of _____ musicians.

MIND-BENDER MATH

5 minutes

QUICK THINK

Directions

Solve the following math problems in five minutes or less.

1. double 12 1/4 =   _____

2. take away 6 from 101 =   _____

3. 16 + 12 + 9 =   _____

4. minutes in 2 1/4 hours =   _____

5. double 14.5 =   _____

6. sum of 96 and 86 =   _____

7. cents in $19.56 =   _____

8. difference between 500 and 156 =   _____

9. half of 108 1/2 =   _____

10. 12 x 10 = 200 – ____   _____

11. months in 6 1/4 years =   _____

12. total days in June, July, and August = _____

5
minutes

DOWN AND ACROSS

Activity

48

Directions

Place the numbers from the box in the blank circles to make each total correct—horizontally and vertically. Use each number once only.

| 2 | 3 | 4 | 5 | 6 | 7 | 8 | 9 |

5 × ( ) ÷ ( ) = 10

× + +

( ) × ( ) ÷ ( ) = 18

÷ − +

( ) + ( ) − ( ) = 4

= = =

6   6   13

5 minutes

ANSWER MATCH

Activity
49

Directions

Look at the left and right sides in the columns below. On each side, there are equations that have the same answer. Draw lines between equations that have the same answer.

MIND-BENDER MATH

12 x 12	5 x 39
7 x 16	6 x 24
9 x 22	1,346 – 912
155 ÷ 5	207 ÷ 9
184 ÷ 8	423 + 446
378 + 540	1,153 – 756
3,865 – 2,996	20 + 11
13 x 15	138 x 9
398 + 447	3,444 ÷ 6
62 x 7	28 x 4
634 – 237	27 x 34
54 x 23	11 x 18
14 x 41	924 – 79

15
minutes

PUZZLING PATTERNS

Activity
50

Directions

Find the next two terms of each sequence. Then look for the answers in the box below. Fill the spaces with the letters for the answers. The resulting words will be the answer to the riddle. (Note: Not every answer has a space below.)

1. 8, 16, 24, 32, _____ , _____
          M   N

2. 1, 8, 27, 64, _____ , _____
           A   E

3. 1, 3, 9, 27, _____ , _____
          S   T

4. 1, 4, 7, 10, _____ , _____
           H   I

5. 1, 1, 2, 3, 5, _____ , _____
             F   H

6. 7, 4, 1, -2, -5, _____ , _____
                 C   D

7. 3, 4.5, 6, 7.5, _____ , _____
                X   Y

8. 6.89, 7, 7.11, 7.22, _____ , _____
                      Q   R

9. 1, 3, 7, 13, 21, _____ , _____
                 K   L

10. 5, -1, 2, -4, -1, _____ , _____
                  G   P

What did the construction worker say when the rabbit stepped onto the forklift?

___ ___ ,   ___ ___ ___ ___   ___ ___
40 10.5   243 13 16 81   16 81

___ ___ ___ ___ ___ ___ ___ ___ ___ ___   ___
-11 216 8 16 48 16 243 216 43 10.5   125

___ ___ ___ ___ — ___ ___ ___ ___ ___ ___ ___
13 125 7.44 216   7.44 125 16 81 16 48 -7

___ ___ ___ ___ ___ ___ ___ ___ ___ ___ !
216 9 -4 216 7.44 16 216 48 -8 216

15
minutes

MATH SNAKES

Activity 51

Directions

Look for "math snakes" that equal 16 in the grid below. The numbers and math signs have to be touching, but they do not have to be in a straight line. You may use a number more than once. Two have been done for you.

34	÷	2	–	1	+	12	+	8	–
–	20	x	5	÷	4	–	9	+	5
24	–	16	x	2	+	6	x	2	x
+	4	+	28	÷	2	x	4	–	4
4	+	6	x	5	+	34	–	4	–
+	6	x	8	÷	3	x	2	+	2
2	x	2	+	5	+	9	÷	3	x
x	14	+	5	÷	11	–	2	÷	3
8	+	4	–	2	x	9	+	3	÷
+	4	+	4	+	9	–	90	+	6

10 minutes

54

MIND-BENDER MATH

PRIME NUMBERS

Activity 52

Directions

Find your way through the maze by coloring only the prime numbers.
You cannot move diagonally.

Start

		30	164	148	128	105	135	117	156
141	151	148	100	112	5	71	97	53	134
164	29	123	114	129	89	158	121	101	147
155	67	106	122	43	109	111	165	7	126
47	139	9	150	113	116	142	104	179	152
3	115	143	130	2	163	99	41	73	102
107	98	159	96	88	127	84	179	120	140
103	144	96	13	163	37	80	229	199	161
59	124	13	163	38	80	160	132	167	110
137	92	131	138	81	160	132	87	157	94
11	157	17	90	154	86	125	119	173	133
145	118	91	166	85	146	77	85		

Finish

15 minutes

MIND-BENDER MATH

FACTOR FUN

Directions

Write the missing factors to complete these factor trees.

1.

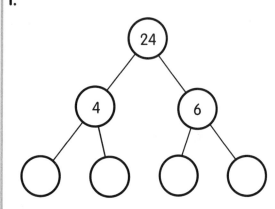

4.

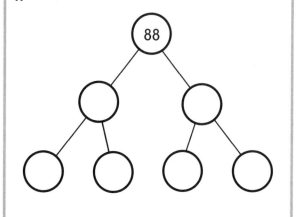

2.

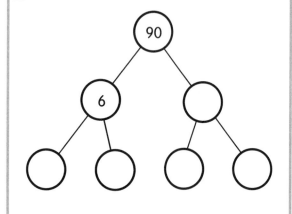

5.

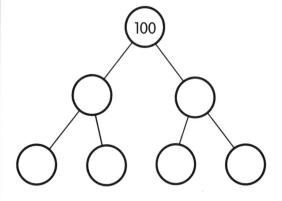

3.

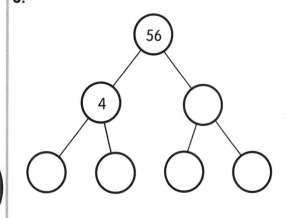

6.

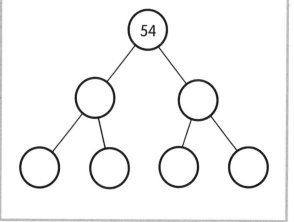

5 minutes

SHAPING UP

Activity
54

Directions

Follow the instructions beside each shape to make some new shapes.

1. Draw four lines to make at least six triangles.

2. Draw two lines to make at least four triangles.

3. Draw three lines to make one rectangle and at least three triangles.

4. Draw three lines to make six triangles.

5. Draw three lines to make two squares and at least four triangles.

MIND-BENDER MATH

5
minutes

COORDINATE CODE

Directions

Use the coordinates to decipher the coded message.

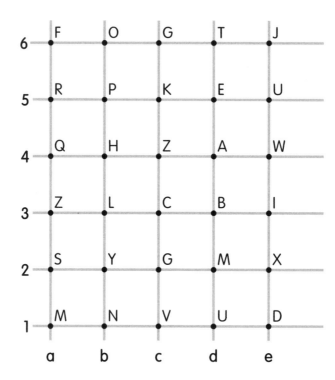

MIND-BENDER MATH

___ ___ ___ ___ ___ ___ ___   ___   ___ ___ ___ ___ ___ ___
(b,5) (a,5) (d,5) (b,5) (d,4) (a,5) (d,5)   (d,4)   (d,2) (d,5) (a,2) (a,2) (d,4) (c,2) (d,5)

___ ___   ___ ___ ___ ___   ___ ___ ___ ___ ___ ___
(d,6) (b,6)   (b,2) (b,6) (e,5) (a,5)   (a,6) (a,5) (e,3) (d,5) (b,1) (e,1)

___ ___ ___ ___ ___   ___ ___ ___
(e,5) (a,2) (e,3) (b,1) (c,2)   (d,6) (b,4) (d,5)

___ ___ ___ ___ ___ ___ ___ ___ ___ ___ ___ ___
(d,4) (b,3) (b,5) (b,4) (d,4) (d,3) (d,5) (d,6) (e,3) (c,3) (d,4) (b,3)

___ ___ ___ ___ ___ ___ ___ ___ ___ ___   ___ ___ ___ ___.
(c,3) (b,6) (b,6) (a,5) (e,1) (e,3) (b,1) (d,4) (d,6) (d,5)   (c,2) (a,5) (e,3) (e,1)

MATH TERMS

Directions

Solve each math problem. Then match the mathematical term on the right that is associated with the circled item on the left. Write the letter on the line.

_____ **1.**
$$\begin{array}{r} 345 \\ -123 \\ \hline \end{array}$$

A. product

_____ **2.** ⬭ x 7 = 35

B. sum

_____ **3.** 72 ÷ 8 = ⬭

C. addend

_____ **4.** ⬭
$$\begin{array}{r} + \ 2,345 \\ \hline 5,889 \end{array}$$

D. difference

_____ **5.** 22 x 4 = ⬭

E. factor

_____ **6.** 35 + 43 = ⬭

F. quotient

_____ **7.**  = ⬭

G. numerator

_____ **8.**  = $\dfrac{}{5}$

H. fraction

_____ **9.**  = $\dfrac{7}{}$ ⬭

I. denominator

10 minutes

NAME _____   DATE _____

DIVISION SKATE

Activity
57

Directions

Which path will correctly take Chris to the skate ramp with a final answer of 23? Calculate all paths and fill in the blank spaces.

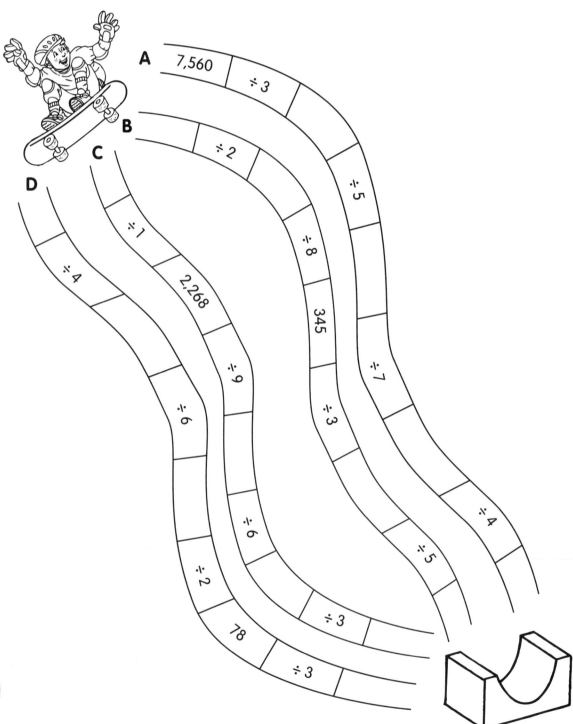

10 minutes

MULTIPLYING DECIMALS

Activity 58

Directions

Solve each multiplication problem. Write each product in the number puzzle. Be sure to include the decimal points in the puzzle.
See #2 Across. It has been done for you.

Across

2. 9.726 x 3 = _____29.178_____

4. 3.82 x 2 = _____

6. 4.2 x 7 = _____

7. 7.3 x 3 = _____

9. 9.8 x 5 = _____

10. .12 x 7 = _____

12. 7.5 x 8 = _____

13. .69 x 6 = _____

14. 8.008 x 7 = _____

17. 8.386 x 4 = _____

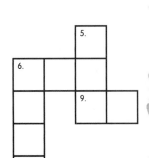

MIND-BENDER MATH

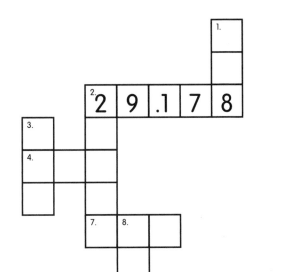

Down

1. .47 x 4 = _____

2. 1.3201 x 2 = _____

3. 5.80 x 3 = _____

5. 2.11 x 4 = _____

6. 7.068 x 3 = _____

8. 6.4 x 2 = _____

11. 9.21 x 5 = _____

13. .54 x 9 = _____

15. 5.95 x 9 = _____

16. .17 x 2 = _____

15 minutes

RIVER CROSSING

Activity
59

Directions

Cross the river by collecting the number of points as you step across on the stones. Try to reach the other side with exactly 5,000,000 points. Color the stones you used.

MIND-BENDER MATH

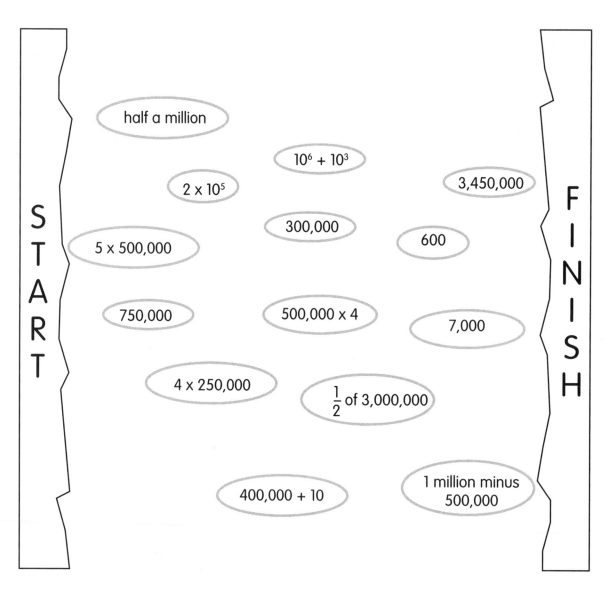

half a million

$10^6 + 10^3$

2 x 10^5

3,450,000

300,000

600

5 x 500,000

750,000

500,000 x 4

7,000

4 x 250,000

$\frac{1}{2}$ of 3,000,000

400,000 + 10

1 million minus 500,000

S T A R T

F I N I S H

10 minutes

62

COLOR SQUARES

Activity
60

Directions

Figure out the answers to the problems below, then color the square containing the answer in the indicated color.

Color	Question	Answer
Red	$8 + 12 + 9 + 7$	
Blue	$5^2 + 4^2$	
Green	prime numbers between 12 and 20	
Pink	$(96 \div 2) - (16 \div 4)$	
Yellow	neither prime nor composite	
Brown	$100 - 26 - 34$	
Orange	$(4 \times 8) - (28 - 11)$	
Purple	$(70 \div 5) + 32$	

MIND-BENDER MATH

1	2	3	4	5	6	7	8	9	10
11	12	13	14	15	16	17	18	19	20
21	22	23	24	25	26	27	28	29	30
31	32	33	34	35	36	37	38	39	40
41	42	43	44	45	46	47	48	49	50
51	52	53	54	55	56	57	58	59	60
61	62	63	64	65	66	67	68	69	70

10
minutes

FRACTION PATH

MIND-BENDER MATH

Directions

From Start, find a path to Finish following the path of **decreasing** fractions or expressions. You may move from one box to another vertically, horizontally, or diagonally. Color the boxes of your path as you go. Use a calculator to compare fractions and decimals.

Start					Finish
1.52	$0.85 + \frac{9}{10}$	$\frac{17}{20} + \frac{3}{4}$	2.1	$2 - \frac{1}{8}$	$\frac{2}{1,000}$
$\frac{11}{12} + \frac{7}{12}$	$\frac{3}{4} + \frac{3}{4}$	1.85	$\frac{15}{16} + \frac{7}{8}$	$3 - 1\frac{7}{8}$	$\frac{10}{100} + \frac{100}{1,000}$
$\frac{7}{8} + \frac{7}{8}$	1.48	$\frac{9}{10} + \frac{1}{2}$	$\frac{38}{100} + \frac{7}{10}$	$2.4 - 0.6$	$1 - \frac{65}{100}$
$1 - 0.45$	$\frac{15}{16} + \frac{1}{2}$	$1 + \frac{25}{100}$	$\frac{11}{12} + \frac{5}{6}$	$\frac{8}{9} + \frac{1}{3}$	$\frac{3}{8} + \frac{1}{16}$
2×0.8	$\frac{17}{20} + 0.15$	$\frac{7}{8} + \frac{1}{2}$	$\frac{5}{8} + \frac{1}{4}$	$\frac{11}{12} - \frac{1}{4}$	$0.74 - 0.19$
$1\frac{3}{7} + \frac{1}{7}$	$\frac{95}{100} + \frac{3}{10}$	$1 - \frac{1}{20}$	110%	$\frac{13}{14}$	99%

15 minutes

WORKING WITH INTEGERS

Directions

Solve each problem. Use the letters next to the problems to solve the riddle at the bottom of the page. Many letters will be used more than once while other letters will not be used at all.

H. 7 + (-5) = _____

Q. -8 + 4 = _____

D. 4 + (-6) = _____

B. -15 + (-3) = _____

F. -28 + 28 = _____

G. -9 – 2 = _____

O. 6 + -9 = _____

W. -7 + -8 = _____

K. -2 + (-4) = _____

Q. -7 – (-3) = _____

X. -15 + (-6) = _____

S. -19 – (-18) = _____

A. 7 – 16 = _____

V. -2 – (-8) = _____

U. 8 – (-3) = _____

E. -9 + (-7) = _____

Y. -2 + 7 = _____

J. -18 + (-3) = _____

Z. (6 - 2) – (-4) = _____

N. 6 - [2 - (-3)] = _____

M. 6 + [2 - (-4)] = _____

I. 10 + 22 + (-7) + (-30) = _____

P. -31 + 62 + (-9) = _____

T. 9 + 24 + (-5) + (-25) = _____

R. -5 + -6 + -9 = _____

L. -20 + (-19) - 2 = _____

C. 5 x 3 – (8 – 6) = _____

Why did the dentist decide to join the army?

___ ___   ___ ___ ___ ___ ___ ___ ___
2 -16   3   2 -3 11 -11 2   3

___ ___   ___ ___ ___ ___ ___
2 -16   -15 -3 11 -41 -2

___ ___   ___   ___ ___ ___ ___
-18 -16   -9   -11 -3 -3 -2

___ ___ ___ ___ ___
-2 -20 -5 -41 -41

___ ___ ___ ___ ___ ___ ___ ___ .
-1 -16 -20 -11 -16 -9 1   3

#2966 101 Activities for Fast Finishers

MIND-BENDER MATH

20 minutes

WHAT'S LEFT?

Activity
63

Directions

Find and cross out all of the listed geometrical terms in the puzzle. When all of the terms have been found, use the remaining letters in order, from top to bottom and left to right, to form an answer to the riddle. The stars in the puzzle represent spaces between words. The first three terms have been done for you.

MIND-BENDER MATH

```
L A S R E V S N A R T V A F T
A E R O I R E T N I A E R A R
R E L G N A I R T ★ T R N P A
E R A U Q S D D T U I T N O G
T N E U R G N O C I ★ E U L C
A P ★ E L G N A A L C X R Y T
L N L X R V O L U M E A ★ G N
I O T T H G E ★ E F D E L O E
U G A E C T E O S I R S G N M
Q A R R S ★ I D U ★ F A N I G
E T O I G N U S T R T B I R E
R N T O E C O N B C ★ I D A S
H E C R R A Y G O T ★ M N L S
O P A D E U R L A G S T O I U
M A R I C ' A V I X A E P M P
B R T O T T T L I N E C S I P
U A O Z A N N A E ★ D H E S L
S L R E N I E N R B I E R D E
E L P P G O M O U S M P R I M
E E N A L P E G S R A T O A E
B L R R E D L A A I R A C M N
I N E T ★ I P I E G Y G S E T
S U L M - M M D M H P O T T A
E H U I O P O I N T N N G E R
C I R C L E C G E O M E T R Y
T N E C A J D A ★ H T G N E L
```

~~Acute~~	Midpoint
~~Adjacent~~	Obtuse
~~Angle~~	Octagon
Area	Parallel
Base	Pentagon
Bisect	Plane
Circle	Point
Compass	Polygon
Complementary	Protractor
Cone	Pyramid
Congruent	Radius
Corresponding	Ray
Cylinder	Rectangle
Decagon	Rhombus
Degree	Right
Diagonal	Ruler
Diameter	Segment
Equilateral	Similar
Exterior	Square
Geometry	Supplementary
Heptagon	Transversal
Hexagon	Trapezoid
Interior	Triangle
Length	Vertex
Line	Vertical
Measure	Volume

20 minutes

Why was the math teacher mad at you?

_____

_____

NAME _____ DATE _____

CROSSNUMBER

Directions

Answer each math problem below. Write each answer in the puzzle.

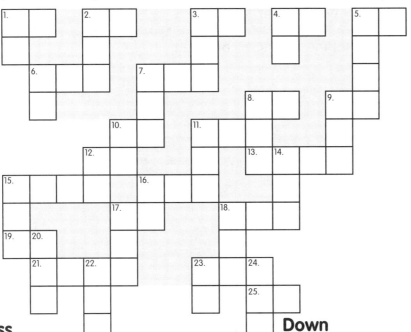

Across

1. $10)\overline{100}$
2. 216 ÷ 6
3. divide 960 by 12
4. 427 ÷ 7
5. $\sqrt{225} \div 1$
6. 3,384 ÷ 6
7. 20 centuries ÷ 4 = ____ years
8. 240 divided by 5
9. $\frac{1}{5}$ of 200
10. largest factor of 81
11. $4)\overline{868}$
12. (62 + 33) ÷ 5
13. $\frac{1}{4}$ of 10,000
15. 90,000 ÷ 10
16. quotient when 1,344 is divided by 7
17. 6 for 36¢. How many for $1.20?
18. 64 x 10 ÷ 4
19. 144 ÷ 12
21. $11)\overline{65,131}$
23. How many 10 cm pieces in 62.2 m?
25. 1, 3, 9, ____ , 81

Down

1. 80 ÷ 8
2. How many groups of 3 in 1,032?
3. 9 pairs of socks at 90¢ per pair
4. divide 536 by 8
5. $49.20 ÷ 4
6. $(6 + 4)^2 \div 2$
7. ____ ÷ 3 = 187
8. (472 x 2) ÷ 2
9. 4,000 ÷ 10
10. 8,900 ÷ 100
11. 1,000 ÷ 5 + 12
12. 260 ÷ 26
14. 171 ÷ 3 x 10
15. 901 ÷ 1
16. How many 12s in 120?
17. average of 125, 183, 270, 266
18. 976 divided by 8
20. $\frac{1}{4}$ of 1,000
22. $\sqrt{36} \div 3 \times 100$
23. 3 centuries ÷ 5 = _____ years
24. 1,338 legs; how many insects?

20 minutes

©Teacher Created Resources 67 #2966 101 Activities for Fast Finishers

FINDING EQUIVALENTS

Activity
65

Directions

Complete the chart below. When you solve the two missing values for each row, write the answers next to the letters. Then write the letters above the answers in the blanks below to solve the riddle. Not all of the letters will be used.

	Fraction	Decimal	Percent
1.	I	.007	L
2.	2/3	A	O
3.	E	.75	B
4.	D	F	6%
5.	U	C	50%
6.	A	$.\overline{5}$	P
7.	1/25	H	I
8.	R	.38	F
9.	N	$.\overline{7}$	M
10.	15/16	O	V
11.	T	W	44%

What does the star peacock of the basketball team expect during a game?

___ ___ ___ ___   ___ ___
5/9 .7% .9375 11/25   .9375 .06

___ ___ ___ ___   — ___ ___
.04 66.7% .9375 55.5%   .7% .667

___ ___ ___   ___ ___ ___   —
5/9 7/9 3/50   .06 .667 7/9

___ ___ ___ ___!
38% 5/9 19/50 3/4

20
minutes

WHAT AM I?

Activity
66

Directions

Read each set of clues to find the mystery numbers. Write the number in its box.

1. I am a five-digit number.
My digits increase in size from the left.
Each digit is different.
My first and fifth digits are square numbers.
My first and fourth digits are cubed numbers.
My second and third digits are consecutive odd numbers.

I am

2. I am a six-digit number.
All my digits are different.
My digits decrease in value from the left.
My second digit is a triangular number.
I am divisible by 10.
My first four digits are even.

I am

3. My number has five digits.
I am a multiple of 11.
My first and fourth digits are the same and are a square number.
My third and fifth digits are prime numbers.
If I was rounded to the nearest hundred thousand I would be 100,000.
My second digit is greater than 7.

I am

4. I have seven digits.
My first two digits make a multiple of 6 and of 9, which is less than 30.
My third and fifth digits are place keepers.
My last two digits are a multiple of 11 and are said to be lucky numbers.
The sum of my digits is 28.

I am

10 minutes

MIND-BENDER MATH

EXPRESSIONS

Activity 67

Directions

Find the letter for each expression that matches each phrase.
To answer the riddle below, write the letter on the blank space
or spaces that match the problem number.

1. a number added to 6
2. 10 decreased by a number
3. 21 plus a number
4. a number divided by 18
5. four times a number
6. four times the sum of a number and two
7. 18 divided by a number
8. a number minus 3
9. a number decreased by 10
10. 11 more than a number
11. a number subtracted from 3
12. a number multiplied by 2
13. the sum of 9 and x
14. the quotient of 9 and a number
15. the product of 9 and a number
16. 9 less than n
17. a number subtracted from 9

D. $9 - n$
R. $18 \div n$
E. $21 + n$
H. $10 - n$
N. $n + 11$
A. $4n$
Y. $n - 3$
O. $2n$
S. $6 + n$
W. $n \div 18$
G. $3 - n$
I. $n - 10$
T. $4(n + 2)$
K. $9 \div n$
U. $9 \times n$
M. $9 + x$
P. $n - 9$

Why did the lady put lipstick on her head?

$\overline{}_{1}\ \overline{}_{2}\ \overline{}_{3}\quad \overline{}_{4}\ \overline{}_{5}\ \overline{}_{1}\quad \overline{}_{6}\ \overline{}_{7}\ \overline{}_{8}\ \overline{}_{9}\ \overline{}_{10}\ \overline{}_{11}$

$\overline{}_{6}\ \overline{}_{12}\quad \overline{}_{13}\ \overline{}_{5}\ \overline{}_{14}\ \overline{}_{3}\quad \overline{}_{15}\ \overline{}_{16}\quad \overline{}_{2}\ \overline{}_{3}\ \overline{}_{7}$

$\overline{}_{13}\ \overline{}_{9}\ \overline{}_{10}\ \overline{}_{17}.$

10 minutes

GRAPHING COORDINATES

Directions

Graph the coordinates below in order from A to H and I to W. Connect each dot with a straight edge as you proceed. (Note: You will go over some line segments more than once.)

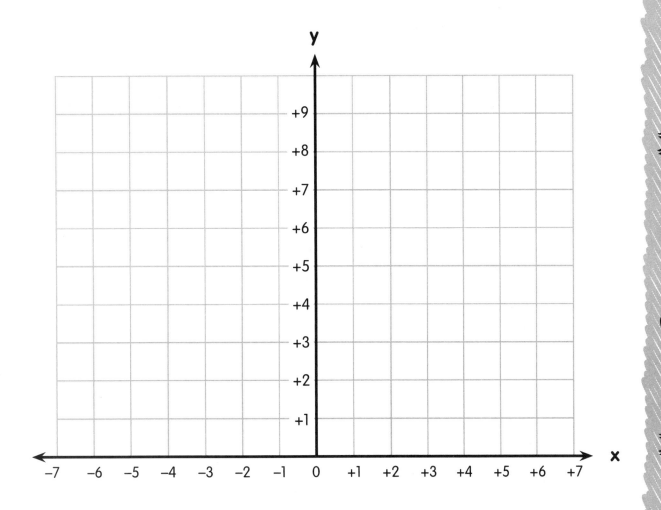

MIND-BENDER MATH

First Shape

A. (+1, +3)	B. (+6, +3)	C. (+6, +8)	D. (+1, +8)	E. (+1, +3)
F. (+6, +8)	G. (+1, +8)	H. (+6, +3)		

Second Shape

I. (−2, +2)	J. (−6, +2)	K. (−7, +5)	L. (−6, +8)	M. (−2, +8)
N. (−1, +5)	O. (−2, +2)	P. (−6, +8)	Q. (−2, +8)	R. (−6, +2)
S. (−7, +5)	T. (−1, +5)	U. (−4, +5)	V. (−4, +8)	W. (−4, +2)

15 minutes

PALINDROMES GALORE

Activity 69

Directions

Every answer in this crossnumber puzzle is a palindrome (number that can be read the same forward and backward). Use a calculator to help you complete the puzzle.

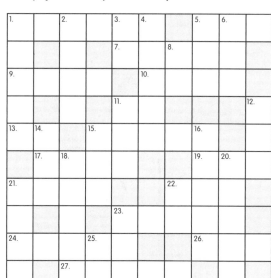

MIND-BENDER MATH

20 minutes

Across

1. $583^2 + (100 - 7 \times 8)$

5. $5^4 - 10^2$

7. $\frac{3}{4}$ of $57,524 - \frac{1}{2}$ of $11,140$

9. $2 \times 3 \times 11 \times 101$

10. $\sqrt{64} \times (500 - 181)$

11. $\frac{1}{20}$ of $1,540$

13. $\frac{3}{11}$ of 121

15. $229 \times \sqrt{256} \times 11$

17. $\frac{1}{2}$ of $8,008 + \frac{1}{3}$ of $9,339$

19. $(279 \div 9) \times (252 \div 18) \times \sqrt{4}$

21. $(39 \times 10 + 4) \times 11$

22. $17 + 209 + 7 + 282$

23. $\frac{7}{8}$ of $100,000 - 8,913$

24. $(60,000 - 35,891) \times 3$

26. Double $(1,589 \div 7)$

27. $5,942 + 17,803 - 11,024$

Down

1. $331 \times 96 + 5,897$

2. $\frac{1}{2}$ of $16,426 + \frac{1}{3}$ of $4,368$

3. $\sqrt{1,089}$

4. $50,000 - (30,000 - 17,273)$

5. 23×5^2

6. $2^3 \times 29$

8. $\sqrt{10,000} - (3^2 \times 5)$

11. $7 \times (4^3 + 37)$

12. $37 \times 2^3 \times 3$

14. $7^2 + 18^2$

15. $\frac{2}{5}$ of $1,035$

16. $19 \times (185 + 132) \times 2^3$

18. 317×43

20. $23,945 + 917 + 31,519 + 9,375$

21. $10,742 - 5,968$

22. $119 - 4^3$

23. $6,993 \div \sqrt{81}$

25. $\sqrt{4} \times \sqrt{121}$

72

SOLVING PROPORTIONS

Activity
70

Directions

Solve each proportion, and then replace the blank spaces in the box below with the variable that matches each answer to solve the riddle. Not all of the letters will be used.

1. $\dfrac{5}{6} = \dfrac{e}{36}$ e = _____

2. $\dfrac{4}{8} = \dfrac{i}{27}$ i = _____

3. $\dfrac{3}{26} = \dfrac{9}{p}$ p = _____

4. $\dfrac{n}{7} = \dfrac{15}{7}$ n = _____

5. $\dfrac{4}{5} = \dfrac{o}{1.25}$ o = _____

6. $\dfrac{3}{8} = \dfrac{27}{d}$ d = _____

7. $\dfrac{L}{8.4} = \dfrac{3}{1.2}$ L = _____

8. $\dfrac{9.3}{r} = \dfrac{.27}{.9}$ r = _____

9. $\dfrac{1.7}{5.1} = \dfrac{.5}{v}$ v = _____

10. $\dfrac{1.1}{3.3} = \dfrac{6.9}{w}$ w = _____

What is the name of the best receiver on the football team?

__ __ __ __   __.
20.7 13.5 21 21   30

__ __ __ __ __ __ __ __
30 1.5 30 31 72 31 1 78

MIND-BENDER MATH

20 minutes

WORD PLAY

Directions

Take one letter from the first word and place it in the second word to form two new words with similar meanings.

Example: curt / cave = cut / carve.

1. flat / pump =   _____ / _____

2. shred / ban =   _____ / _____

3. boast / hip =   _____ / _____

4. blare / bad =   _____ / _____

5. snap / lumber =   _____ / _____

6. hope / lap =   _____ / _____

7. bread / peal =   _____ / _____

8. scream / scape =   _____ / _____

9. stalk / peak =   _____ / _____

10. pierce / pat =   _____ / _____

5
minutes

CAREER PLATES

Activity

72

Directions

A car license plate can tell something about its owner. Decode these plates to reveal clues about the owner's career.

1.
   DRTOOTH

   _____

2.
   IFXPETS

   _____

3.
   LUV2SNG

   _____

4.
   STAR4ME

   _____

5.
   WWW4YOU

   _____

6.
   NOFIRES

   _____

7.
   LVS2TCH

   _____

8.
   FOTOIDO

   _____

9.
   SEWWHAT

   _____

10.
    FLYGIRL

    _____

11.
    HSE4SLE

    _____

12.
    RNNRBOY

    _____

BEYOND BRAINY

10 minutes

MEMORY TEST

Activity
13

Directions

Study the objects below for two minutes. When time is up, cover them and write down as many as you can remember.

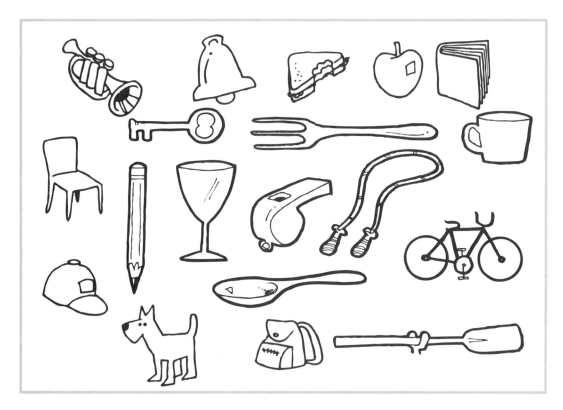

1. _____
2. _____
3. _____
4. _____
5. _____
6. _____
7. _____
8. _____
9. _____
10. _____

11. _____
12. _____
13. _____
14. _____
15. _____
16. _____
17. _____
18. _____
19. _____

BEYOND BRAINY

5 minutes

76

BODY LANGUAGE

Activity
74

Directions

Fill in the blanks with parts of the body to complete the common phrases.

1. get a _____ in the door

2. get to the _____ of the matter

3. all _____ on deck

4. with your _____ to the wall

5. by the _____ of one's _____

6. keep a stiff upper_____

7. see _____ to _____

8. a lump in the _____

9. out on a _____

10. _____ and _____ above the rest

11. stick your _____ out

12. _____ flop

13. a _____ watch

14. to go in one _____ and out the other

15. nothing but _____ and _____

BEYOND BRAINY

10
minutes

TRANSPORTATION

Activity
15

Directions

Hidden in the word search are 22 different types of transportation. The first letter of each one is given below in alphabetical order. Find them in the puzzle and write their names on the lines.

BEYOND BRAINY

S	R	S	B	Z	T	R	U	C	K	H	O	W	K	W
S	B	E	P	O	Q	O	R	Q	Q	F	N	M	Z	H
T	O	C	E	A	N	L	I	N	E	R	T	M	I	Y
A	A	C	S	I	C	L	I	A	R	O	N	O	M	D
N	O	O	U	R	H	E	L	I	C	O	P	T	E	R
K	E	G	B	P	Q	R	S	W	E	S	V	O	Q	O
E	L	V	W	L	U	S	R	H	V	K	M	R	R	F
R	C	Q	A	A	I	K	Q	T	U	A	O	C	O	O
O	Y	N	Y	N	W	A	M	M	S	T	X	Y	T	I
K	C	A	R	E	V	T	S	Q	A	E	T	C	A	L
N	I	A	R	T	T	E	L	L	U	B	A	L	V	K
Y	B	G	E	P	G	S	A	R	I	O	V	E	E	I
R	W	V	F	R	I	C	K	S	H	A	W	U	L	Z
F	N	Y	G	L	S	U	B	M	A	R	I	N	E	R
C	B	M	R	E	A	S	K	H	H	D	B	F	Q	D

1. A _____

2. B _____

3. B _____ T _____

4. C _____

5. E _____

6. E _____

7. F _____

8. H _____

9. H _____

10. M _____

11. M _____

12. O _____ L _____

13. R _____

14. R _____ S _____

15. S _____

16. S _____

17. S _____ S _____

18. S _____

19. S _____

20. S _____

21. T _____

22. T _____

20 minutes

MAP MADNESS

Directions

Do you see Tim? He is lost! Follow the directions to get him back on track. Mark his ending spot with an **X**.

1. Take Abbott St. toward Water St.

2. Turn onto W. Cordova St. toward Howe St.

3. Go left on Richards St.

4. Go west on W. Georgia St.

5. Turn onto Howe St. toward W. Hastings St.

6. End at the corner of Dunsmuir St.

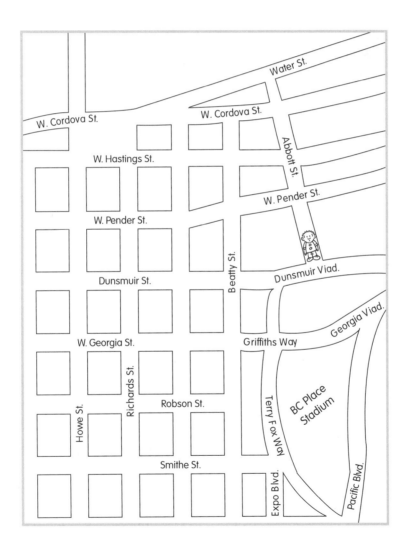

BEYOND BRAINY

Bonus: Now, write directions telling Tim how to get to BC Place Stadium from his current location. _____

_____

10 minutes

IDIOMS

Activity
17

Directions

Fill in the blanks with the words in the box to complete the idioms. Then use the missing words to complete the crossword puzzle. 12 Across has been done for you.

arm	nine
up	bug
beans	heels
world	air
milk	oats
apple	cherries
down	heaven
dollars	heart
dumps	

Across

3. On top of the _____ — feeling very happy

5. Thumbs _____ — approval

7. Snug as a _____ in a rug — comfortable, safe and secure

8. On cloud _____ — very happy and joyous

9. _____ of your eye — someone that is loved and adored

11. Walking on _____ — to be very happy and excited

12. Bowl of _____cherries_____ — a wonderful, happy situation

14. Feel your _____ — to be in high spirits and act in a proud way

16. Kick up your _____ — to celebrate and have a good time

Down

1. Feel like a million _____ — feel wonderful

2. Broken _____ — very unhappy

4. Down in the _____ — sad and depressed

6. Eat your _____ out — to feel unhappy about a hopeless situation

7. Full of _____ — lively and happy

10. Don't cry over spilt _____ — you should not be sad about something that is in the past or something that you cannot do anything about

13. Seventh _____ — the best of all possible places

15. Shot in the _____ — something that lifts your spirits

LOSING LINES

Directions

You can make 14 squares using the lines in the first shape. Cross out eight lines to leave only two squares. You can make 10 triangles using the lines in the second shape. Cross out four lines to leave only four triangles.

1.

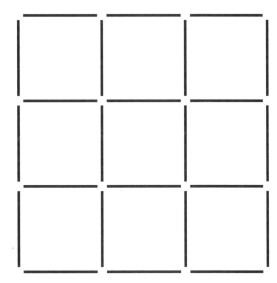

2.

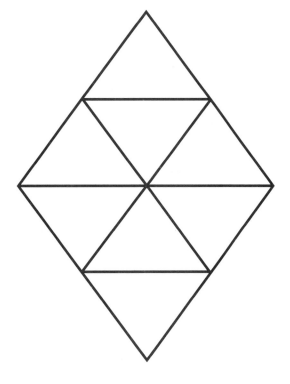

BEYOND BRAINY

5 minutes

Changing Letters

Directions

Change the letters in the starting clue by following the clues below. When moving letters, the remaining letters will move over. When you finish, you will reveal the name of the U.S. president the clue refers to.

Starting Clue: SERVED FOUR TERMS

1. Move the F to the beginning.

   ___ ___ ___ ___ ___ ___ ___ ___ ___ ___ ___ ___ ___ ___ ___ ___

2. Move the T to the end.

   ___ ___ ___ ___ ___ ___ ___ ___ ___ ___ ___ ___ ___ ___ ___ ___

3. Change the first S from the right to an L.

   ___ ___ ___ ___ ___ ___ ___ ___ ___ ___ ___ ___ ___ ___ ___ ___

4. Add 2 Os between the first E from the right and the second R from the right.

   ___ ___ ___ ___ ___ ___ ___ ___ ___ ___ ___ ___ ___ ___ ___ ___

5. Move the first R from the left two spaces to the left.

   ___ ___ ___ ___ ___ ___ ___ ___ ___ ___ ___ ___ ___ ___ ___ ___

6. Move the S to the 6th space from the right.

   ___ ___ ___ ___ ___ ___ ___ ___ ___ ___ ___ ___ ___ ___ ___ ___

7. Change the second E from the left to a K.

   ___ ___ ___ ___ ___ ___ ___ ___ ___ ___ ___ ___ ___ ___ ___ ___

8. Exchange the first E from the left and the M.

   ___ ___ ___ ___ ___ ___ ___ ___ ___ ___ ___ ___ ___ ___ ___ ___

9. Delete the first R from the right.

   ___ ___ ___ ___ ___ ___ ___ ___ ___ ___ ___ ___ ___ ___ ___

10. Move the V between the double Es.

    ___ ___ ___ ___ ___ ___ ___ ___ ___ ___ ___ ___ ___ ___ ___

11. Delete the first two vowels from the left.

    ___ ___ ___ ___ ___ ___ ___ ___ ___ ___ ___ ___ ___

12. Add the word AN between the 2nd and 3rd letters from the left.

    ___ ___ ___ ___ ___ ___ ___ ___ ___ ___ ___ ___ ___ ___ ___

13. Reverse the 5th and 6th letters from the left.

    ___ ___ ___ ___ ___ ___ ___ ___ ___ ___ ___ ___ ___ ___ ___

14. Change the M to an L.

    ___ ___ ___ ___ ___ ___ ___ ___ ___ ___ ___ ___ ___ ___ ___

15. Add the word IN between the 5th and 6th consonants from left.

    ___ ___ ___ ___ ___ ___ ___ ___ ___ ___ ___ ___ ___ ___ ___ ___ ___

BEFORE AND AFTER

Activity 80

Directions

Write a word on the line so that it makes a new word or phrase with the word(s) in front and the word(s) after. The first one has been done for you.

1.	spelling	__bee__	hive
2.	isn't it	_____	child
3.	green	_____	nail
4.	free	_____	shake
5.	ceiling	_____	fare
6.	ginger	_____	basket
7.	tennis	_____	room
8.	paper	_____	board
9.	on the	_____	catcher
10.	ready, set	_____	for it
11.	good for	_____	got it
12.	cross	_____	search

BEYOND BRAINY

5 minutes

Same Letters

Directions

Make a list of words that begin and end with the same letter.
How many can you think of in 10 minutes?

A _____

B _____

C _____

D _____

E _____

F _____

G _____

H _____

I _____

J _____

K _____

L _____

M _____

N _____

O _____

P _____

Q _____

R _____

S _____

T _____

U _____

V _____

W _____

X _____

Y _____

Z _____

BEYOND BRAINY

10 minutes

CAMP CHIPPEWA

Activity
82

Directions

Russ Smith, the camp counselor, and seven boys from his cabin are sitting on blankets around the campfire, roasting marshmallows and telling stories. Using the diagram and the clues below, determine where everyone is sitting. Write their names on the correct lines.

Clues:

- Jeff is sitting on the blanket between Zac and Andrew.
- Danny is sitting between Alan and Ryan.
- The counselor is sitting at the top of the circle of blankets.
- Zac is not sitting next to Russ.
- Mark is to Russ's right.
- Ryan is sitting across from the counselor.

Beyond Brainy

```
                    _____

                     ┌─────┐
                     │  1  │
          ┌─────┐    └─────┘    ┌─────┐
 _____  │  8  │               │  2  │  _____
          └─────┘               └─────┘

          ┌─────┐               ┌─────┐
 _____  │  7  │      🔥       │  3  │  _____
          └─────┘               └─────┘

          ┌─────┐               ┌─────┐
 _____  │  6  │    ┌─────┐    │  4  │  _____
          └─────┘    │  5  │    └─────┘
                     └─────┘

                    _____
```

10 minutes

NAME IN A NAME

Activity
83

Directions

Each of the following names can be found within one of the 50 U.S. state or capital names. Can you think of the states or capitals whose names contain the names listed below?

1. Carol _____

2. Lulu _____

3. Jeff _____

4. Diana _____

5. Tex _____

6. Paul _____

7. Kent _____

8. Art _____

9. Helen _____

10. Jack _____

11. Rich _____

12. Ida _____

13. Trent _____

14. Frank _____

15. Cal _____

16. June _____

17. Louis _____

18. Mary _____

19. Del _____

20. Charles _____

21. Ken _____

22. Anna _____

BEYOND BRAINY

15 minutes

HIDDEN ANIMALS

Activity
84

Directions

Hidden in each sentence are three or four animal names. Can you find them? Circle them and write their names on the lines.

Example: Hel p ig loos! ➔ pig

1. Bingo attendance feels lugubrious tonight.

_____

2. We need a bigger billboard with the blob's terrible ooze branded on it.

_____

3. Unfortunately, the intro utilizes expandable balloons.

_____

4. Eggshell amassed makes the compost rich—it's not complicated!

_____

5. The promo used a card in Alaska to ask unkind questions.

_____

6. Pro bingo players made lemon, Key lime pie for the fortunate cowboy.

_____

7. Thor Seville and Ratchel Stern's friend was part of an old, eerie play.

_____

10 minutes

CLUELESS NUMBERS

Activity
85

Directions

Without any clues to help you, write the numbers from the box in the number puzzle. Three have been placed for you. Be sure to use a pencil!

121,109	310,454	410,228	539,975	951,414
227,116	334,107	461,061	638,720	956,637
288,109	358,123	461,597	876,674	958,861

3 3 4 1 0 7

4 6 1 5 9 7

2 8 8 1 0 9

10 minutes

NAME _____ DATE _____

AMAZING ANAGRAMS

Directions

The two blank spots in each sentence need to be replaced by words.
The missing words are anagrams. This means that one word can be
formed by rearranging the letters of the other. The blanks in each
sentence indicate the number of letters in each word. Fill in the missing
words. The first one has been done for you.

1. They grew __l__ __i__ __m__ __e__ trees on a __m__ __i__ __l__ __e__ of their property.

2. The man ran at a steady __ __ __ __ __ even though he was wearing a __ __ __ __ __.

3. Although she said it wasn't a big __ __ __ __ __ , Gloria was thrilled to have the
   __ __ __ __ __ in the theatrical production.

4. With the __ __ __ __ __ he stole from the safe, he bought a new __ __ __ __ __.

5. The dancer swinging the __ __ __ __ __ has a bad case of __ __ __ __ __ on her face.

6. Shakespeare was an English __ __ __ __ __ who most likely didn't wear __ __ __ __ __
   clothing.

7. The fangs on the __ __ __ __ __ rattlesnake looked so __ __ __ __ __ that the fearful man
   ran away.

8. The gift is so small that it __ __ __ __ __ in his __ __ __ __ __.

9. The chef composed a fruit salad of __ __ __ __ __ __ __ __ , apples, and sweetened
   __ __ __ __ __ __ __ __.

10. All her __ __ __ __ __ , she wanted a fingernail __ __ __ __ __.

11. Will you __ __ __ __ __ over this book as you swing from this __ __ __ __ __ ?

BEYOND BRAINY

20
minutes

HIDDEN MEANINGS

Directions

Explain the meaning of each box.

Activity 87

cycle
cycle
cycle

1. _____

5. _____

milonelion

9. _____

Me Quit!

2. _____

date
date

6. _____

GO   IT
IT
IT
IT

10. _____

3. _____

7. _____

S L O W

11. _____

AGEBEAUTY

4. _____

DECI   SION

8. _____

12. _____

10 minutes

RIDDLE TIME

Activity
88

Directions

Fill in the spaces to make words that fit the definition. The circled letters from top to bottom spell out the answer to the following riddle:

What do you get if you cross a lunch box and a school book?

1. before second 〇 __ __ __ __

2. by oneself __ __ 〇 __ __

3. yarn from sheep __ 〇 __ __

4. no lights 〇 __ __ __ __

5. very large meal 〇 __ __ __ __

6. opposite of top __ 〇 __ __ __

7. house entrance __ __ __ 〇 __

8. found in the sky __ 〇 __ __ __

9. capital city of Virginia __ __ __ 〇 __ __ __ __

10. child's plaything __ __ 〇 __

11. swallow quickly __ 〇 __ __ __

12. rules for good language 〇 __ __ __ __ __ __

13. head covering 〇 __ __ __

14. small rug __ __ 〇 __

BEYOND BRAINY

10 minutes

GENERAL TRIVIA

Activity

89

Directions

Answer as many general trivia questions below as you can in five minutes.

1. A carnivorous animal eats _____ .

2. The young of a deer is called a _____ .

3. The primary colors are red, blue, and _____ .

4. A Chihuahua is a kind of _____ .

5. The name Bill is short for _____ .

6. The terms tee, iron, and green are associated with the sport of _____ .

7. The _____ is also known as the king of the jungle.

8. A decagon has _____ sides.

9. Mutton is the meat of a _____ .

10. What type of creature is Black Beauty? _____

11. What did Cinderella lose at the ball? _____

12. What two colors can you mix to make green? _____

13. What is the name given to the fruit of the oak tree? _____

14. What relation is a girl to her father's brother? _____

5
minutes

15. In what position is the red light on a traffic light? _____

LETTER BOXES

Activity
90

Directions

For each set, put the letters A, B, C, D, E, F, G, H, and I in the boxes according to the clues beside each one.

1. • D, E, and G are in the same column, and none of these touch B.

   • I, H, and G are in the same row, and none of these touch B.

   • D, B, and F are in the same row.

   • F, A, and H are in the same column.

2. • The word *bag* is spelled horizontally (left-to-right), and the word *had* is spelled vertically (top-to-bottom).

   • The vowels are all along the same diagonal.

   • From top-to-bottom, one column reads E-B-F.

3. • Reading clockwise around the outside, you can spell the words *bed* and *hag*, but these words are not touching. (There is at least one letter between these words.)

   • A diagonal spells *ace*.

   • F is above G and A.

   • I is below D and E.

15
minutes

ANIMAL FAMILIES

Activity
91

Directions

Fill in the blanks in the chart to name the different members of each animal family. You may need to research some of the answers.

	Animal	Male	Female	Young	Group
1.	fox				skulk
2.	goat	billy (buck)			
3.	whale		cow		
4.			lioness	cub	
5.			doe	joey	
6.	sheep	ram			
7.	cattle				herd (drove)
8.	seal		cow		
9.				piglet	herd
10.	ostrich				flock
11.			hen		flock
12.			goose		gaggle

BEYOND BRAINY

20
minutes

FAMOUS QUOTE

Activity 92

Directions

Answer each U.S.A. trivia question below. Then fill in the code with the correct letters to reveal a famous quote. You may need to research some of the answers.

1. If Lincoln was president before Cleveland, circle D. If not, circle T.

2. If the Statue of Liberty was given to the U.S. by England, circle E. If not, circle B.

3. If Washington lived in the White House, circle L. If not, circle H.

4. If Kennedy's face is on the half-dollar, circle V. If not, circle S.

5. If Robert E. Lee was a Union general, circle A. If not, circle Y.

6. If Kansas is east of the Rockies, circle O. If not, circle I.

7. If Grover Cleveland was both the 22nd and 24th president, circle A. If not, circle P.

8. If Miss Liberty is holding the book of laws in her left hand, circle M. If not, circle N.

9. If Houston is the capital of Texas, circle L. If not, circle G.

10. If Betsy Ross is said to have made the U.S. flag, circle L. If not, circle M.

11. If Eisenhower's nickname was Ike, circle E. If not, circle T.

12. If there are 103 rooms in the White House, circle T. If not, circle R.

13. If there are more red stripes than white stripes on the U.S. flag, circle T. If not, circle S.

14. If Ben Franklin's face is on Mt. Rushmore, circle L. If not, circle I.

"
___ ___ ___ ___   ___ ___   ___ ___ ___ ___ ___ ___ ___
 9 14   4 11   8 11   10 14   2 11 12 13   5

"
___ ___   ___ ___ ___ ___   ___ ___   ___ ___ ___ ___ ___.
 6 12   9 14   4 11   8 11   1 11   7 13   3

15. Who said these famous words?_____

20 minutes

POTLUCK DINNER

Activity
93

Directions

The Potluck Dinner Club is held every Friday night at 6:30. Read the clues to find the time each member arrived as well as the food item that he or she brought. Mark the chart to help you.

	5:45	6:00	6:15	6:30	6:45	Dessert	Rolls	Salad	Soda	Spaghetti
Betty										
Charlie										
Heidi										
Paul										
Roland										

BEYOND BRAINY

Clues:

- Roland was late for dinner.
- Paul arrived before the person who brought the spaghetti.
- Charlie's rolls were still warm when he arrived.
- Heidi arrived right on time.

- Paul didn't bring the salad or the soda.
- Betty brought the spaghetti and Heidi brought the salad.
- Betty arrived at 6:15 and Paul arrived before Charlie.

1. Betty arrived at _____ and brought the _____ .
2. Charlie arrived at _____ and brought the _____ .
3. Heidi arrived at _____ and brought the _____ .
4. Paul arrived at _____ and brought the _____ .
5. Roland arrived at _____ and brought the _____ .

10 minutes

GEOGRAPHY SANDWICHES

Activity 94

Directions

Sandwiches are made with two pieces of bread and a filling in the middle. In these geography sandwiches, you are given the "bread" but not the "filling." Study a globe or a map of the world to make a proper sandwich.

1. North America _____ Europe

2. Northern Hemisphere _____ Southern Hemisphere

3. Australia _____ New Zealand

4. Europe _____ Asia

5. Africa _____ Australia

6. North America _____ South America

7. Eastern Hemisphere _____ Western Hemisphere

8. Australia _____ Antarctica

9. Europe _____ Africa

10. Australia _____ South America

11. South America _____ Africa

12. Tropic of Cancer _____ Tropic of Capricorn

13. Africa _____ Asia

14. South America _____ Antarctica

15. Asia _____ North America

BEYOND BRAINY

15 minutes

FAMILY FEAST

Directions

Eight people are gathered around the table at Ralph and Mary Johnson's house for a family feast. Read the clues below and determine the name of the person sitting at each place and his or her favorite food.

Guest List

Angie	Mary	Jeffrey
Johnny	Bill	Susie
Ann	Ralph	

Food List

corn	potatoes	ham
pie	green beans	turkey
stuffing	bread rolls	

- Ralph is at the head of the table, and he doesn't like corn.
- No male sits beside another male.
- Angie and Jeffrey are brother and sister; Johnny and Susie are also brother and sister. Each brother and sister pair sits side-by-side on the same side of the table.
- The person who likes ham sits to Ralph's right at the table.
- Bill's wife, Ann, sits to his left at the table. Ralph's wife loves stuffing.
- Susie sits to Bill's right and across from the person who loves green beans. Susie loves bread.
- Jeffrey is a meat lover, and he can't wait for the turkey to be carved.
- Two males love pie and corn, and they sit across the table from each other.

2. Name: _____
Food: _____

3. Name: _____
Food: _____

4. Name: _____
Food: _____

5. Name: _____
Food: _____

1. Head of the Table
Name: _____
Food: _____

8. Name: _____
Food: _____

7. Name: _____
Food: _____

6. Name: _____
Food: _____

15 minutes

BEYOND BRAINY

NAME THE PRO TEAMS

Directions

In the top half, write the professional sports team whose name has the opposite meaning of the given word. In the bottom half, write the professional sports team whose name rhymes with the given word. You may need to research some of the answers.

NFL = National Football League	NBA = National Basketball Association
MLB = Major League Baseball	NHL = National Hockey League

1. Dwarfs _____ NFL

2. Peacemakers _____ NBA

3. Sinners _____ NFL

4. Cowgirls _____ NFL

5. Confederates _____ MLB

6. Queens _____ NBA

7. Moons _____ NBA

8. Coolness _____ NBA

9. Bears _____ NBA

10. Tame _____ NHL

11. Dangers _____ MLB

12. Skins _____ MLB

13. Tubs _____ MLB

14. Volts _____ NFL

15. Sets _____ NFL

16. Hams _____ NFL

17. Towns _____ NFL

18. Pockets _____ NBA

19. Slippers _____ NBA

20. Cornets _____ NBA

BEYOND BRAINY

15 minutes

PRESIDENTIAL CRYPTOGRAM

Activity 97

Directions

In the puzzle below, each letter of the alphabet stands for another letter. You must break the code to solve this cryptogram. Part of the code is given in the box.

Beyond Brainy

N = A	R = E	V = I	B = O	H = U

"
V Q B   F B Y R Z A Y L   F J R N E

G U N G   V   J V Y Y   S N V G U S H Y Y L

R K R P H G R   G U R   B S S V P R   B S

C E R F V Q R A G   B S   G U R   H A V G R Q

F G N G R F '   N A Q   J V Y Y   G B

G U R   O R F G   B S   Z L   N O V Y V G L '

C E R F R E I R '   C E B G R P G '   N A Q

Q R S R A Q   G U R   P B A F G V G H G V B A

B S   G U R   H A V G R Q   F G N G R F "

20 minutes

WHAT'S THE MESSAGE?

Directions

Use the "phone code" to spell out messages for these famous people. Check the numbers against the letters on a phone pad and figure out an appropriate word that is spelled by them. The first one has been done for you.

1. George Washington   765-3437   _____soldier_____

2. Jonas Salk   822-2463   _____

3. Helen Keller   272-4553   _____

4. Tommy Lasorda   363-4377   _____

5. Amelia Earhart   284-2867   _____

6. Kristi Yamaguchi   752-8464   _____

7. George Washington Carver   732-6887   _____

8. Judy Blume and Beverly Cleary   288-4677   _____

9. Fred Astaire   326-2464   _____

10. Ted Kennedy   736-2867   _____

11. Marie Curie   243-6478   _____

BEYOND BRAINY

15 minutes

STICKER TRADING

Activity

Directions

Lyndsay, Juliana, Jon, Steve, and Morgan collect and trade stickers. When they began trading this morning, each student had five stickers of the same pattern. Each student's stickers were different from everyone else's stickers. Any student who received a sticker in trade got to keep that sticker. All students end up with five stickers each. What combination of stickers does each person have at the end of the day? Use the space below to chart the sticker trading and record your answer.

Clues:

- Jon began with five dog stickers and traded stickers with Steve, Lyndsay, and Juliana.
- Morgan began with five balloon stickers. She traded one balloon sticker with each other girl, and one with Steve.
- Lyndsay had five cat stickers. She traded one with Jon and one with Morgan.
- Steve traded one of his planet stickers for a sticker in the shape of an owl.

	🐕	🎈	🐱	🪐	🦉
Lyndsay					
Juliana					
Jon					
Steve					
Morgan					

10 minutes

IN AND OUT

Activity 100

Directions

Reggie cannot join the Ruler Club unless he collects enough inches to make exactly one yard. He must enter the maze at one of the "IN" signs. He can only enter each space once. On the path where there are no arrows he can go in either direction. Help him join the club by coloring the path he must take.

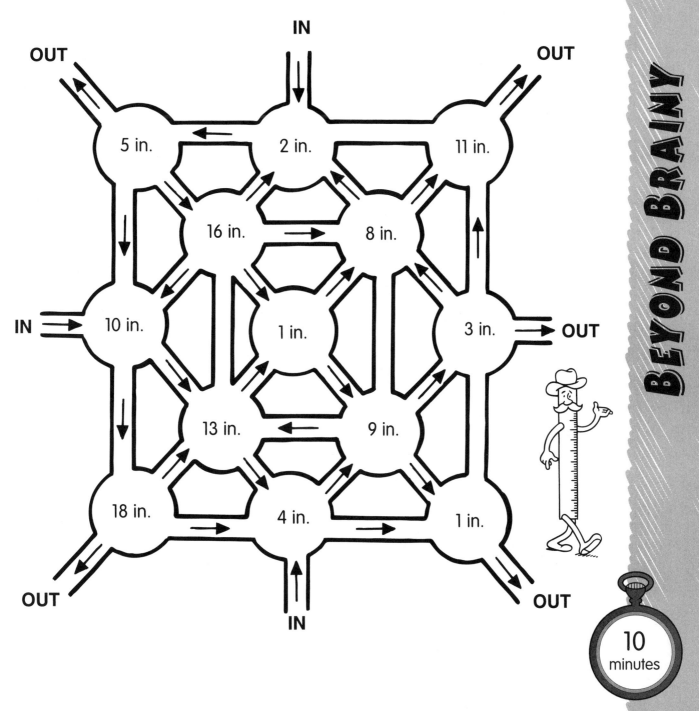

BEYOND BRAINY

10 minutes

COMPLETE A WORD

Directions

Use the 26 letters of the alphabet to complete the words in each box below. Use each letter only one time in each box. Cross off the letters as you use them.

A B C D E F G H I J K L M N O P Q R S T U V W X Y Z

Box 1

1. __ A __ Z

2. __ U I E __

3. __ U __ K Y

4. __ - R __ Y

5. __ I O __ __ N

6. __ A __ __ F U L

7. __ R O __ __

8. __ E __ __ A T

9. __ __ __ A L A

10. __ O L A __

11. __ O R C __ P I N E

Box 2

12. __ R O __ I T

13. B A __ C O N __

14. D __ F E N __

15. R E __ U __ R E

16. __ Y __ T E R I O __ S

17. L A U __ __ __ T E __

18. __ A C __ E T

19. E __ __ __ __ T L Y

20. __ O __ E L

21. C __ N S O __ A N __

22. __ E __ R A

Answer Key

Activity 1
Answers will vary.
Possibilities include: bat, bar, dear, tin, tins, oat, sat, star, strap, trap, bare, ear, tire, soar, part, dirt, bride, tide, print, red, etc.

Activity 2
1. cook
2. sock
3. crab
4. oak
5. boar
6. cobra
7. rock
8. car
9. park
10. cop
11. crook
12. carp

Activity 3
1. ant
2. ill
3. test
4. chin
5. pear
6. tent
7. ate
8. low
9. late
10. up

Activity 4
Answers may vary.
Possibilities include:
1. GIRL, gill, mill, mall, MALE
2. SPIN, spit, spot, slot, PLOT
3. DIET, dirt, dart, dare, CARE
4. WALLS, wills, tills, tiles, tiler, TIGER

Activity 5
1. empty
2. wheel
3. smile, limes
4. found
5. daisy
6. camel
7. fever
8. party
9. habit
10. storm
11. bacon
12. group

13. horse, shore
14. speed, deeps
15. mined, denim
16. angry, rangy
17. mouth
18. write
19. train
20. beetle

Activity 6
1. wheels
2. toffee
3. bubble
4. ballroom
5. summer
6. committee
7. button
8. umbrella
9. terrified
10. disagree
11. letter
12. spoon
13. cabbage
14. pepper
15. teens
16. middle

Activity 7
Group 1: microwave, carpenter, reconstruct, disobey, hemisphere, estimate, nucleus, allowance, parallel, fiesta
Group 2: wonderful, impressive, unravel, tragedy, livelihood, boundary, government, specialize, vigorous, official

Activity 8
1. head start
2. tailgate
3. headline
4. tailor
5. headquarters
6. taillight
7. headache
8. tail end
9. headway
10. tailspin
11. headband
12. tailback
13. head over heels
14. tailpipe
15. headlight

Activity 9
Across
2. short
4. tall
5. still
7. side
8. solution
11. supply
12. spring
13. sure
15. teacher
16. strange
17. space
18. stand

Down
1. sight
2. small
3. tell
5. single
6. sign
7. stay
8. similar
9. suppose
10. step
11. system
13. spread
14. stop
17. sum

Activity 10
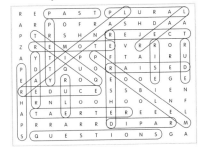

1. problem
2. rational
3. rise
4. rapid
5. real
6. plural
7. rule
8. rude
9. refreshed
10. raised
11. past
12. pretty
13. perhaps
14. quiet
15. remote
16. retreat
17. ready
18. reduce
19. reject
20. questions

Activity 11
1. heard
2. naught
3. center
4. draper
5. sister
6. mouse
7. dribble
8. money
9. hinge
10. latter
11. bleed
12. nature

ANSWER KEY (cont.)

Activity 12
1. soap
2. egg
3. time
4. cream
5. bomb
6. bag
7. flash
8. cart
9. light
10. hall
11. apple
12. pen
13. horse
14. love
15. eye

Activity 13
1. toucan—French; from the sound the birds make
2. chocolate—Aztec; means "bitter water"
3. gazette—Italian; named for a coin used to buy newspapers
4. spaghetti—Italian; means "thin string" or "twine"
5. yacht—Dutch; means "hunt" or "hunting"
6. curry—Tamil; means "sauce"
7. dandelion—French; means "lion's tooth"
8. anthology—Greek; means "flower-gathering"

Activity 14
Red (large): extensive, vast, gargantuan, gigantic, spacious, huge, mammoth, monstrous, massive, colossal, giant

Blue (small): shrunken, stunted, puny, shriveled, wee, dwarfish, trivial, meager, minute, slight, tiny

Yellow (remaining): bellowed, argued, grumbled, replied, groaned, recited, complained, inquired, declared, stammered

The yellow words are variations of the word "said."

Activity 15
Answers will vary.
Possibilities include: blast, boast, beast, boost, burst, coast, chest, crest, crust, exist, feast, first, frost, ghost, heist, joust, least, moist, quest, roast, toast, trust, twist, waist, worst, wrist, yeast

Activity 16
1. except
2. effect
3. capitol
4. counsel
5. imply
6. latter
7. already
8. stationary
9. precede
10. birth
11. weather
12. annual
13. disposition
14. moral
15. isle

Activity 17
1. startling, starting, staring, string, sting, sing, sin, in, I
2. cheated, heated, hated, hate, ate (or hat), at, a
3. cremated, created, create, crate, rate, rat, at, a
4. sprints, prints, pints (or print), pint, pin, in, I

Activity 18
1. license
2. familiar
3. a lot
4. calendar
5. vacuum
6. weird
7. foreign
8. rhythm
9. embarrass
10. appropriate
11. accommodate
12. privilege
13. guarantee
14. irrelevant
15. separate

Activity 19
1. had, would, have
2. did, could
3. am, will
4. were
5. did
6. can
7. was
8. has, can
9. do, are, can
10. had

Activity 20
1. in
2. on
3. beneath
4. on
5. around
6. during
7. across
8. between
9. inside
10. outside

For #11–20, accept appropriate answers. Possibilities include:
11. under
12. across
13. under
14. over
15. At
16. up
17. from
18. beneath
19. in
20. inside

Activity 21
1. assent, ascent
2. course, strait
3. coarse
4. compliment
5. cite
6. taut
7. there, their
8. lesson, lessen
9. presence, presents
10. passed, past

ANSWER KEY (cont.)

Activity 22
1. roster
2. surplus
3. classic
4. synopsis
5. amnesia
6. Alabama
7. blurb
8. exercise
9. penmanship
10. abracadabra
11. erase
12. Australia
13. eagle
14. talent
15. doubled
16. knock
17. hatch
18. greeting
19. millennium
20. recover

Activity 23
1. clap, slap, swap, sway, away
2. ink, inn, ion, ton, ten, pen
3. ring, rind, bind, band, hand
4. game, same, sale, bale, ball
5. hand, band, bond, fond, food, foot
6. malt, male, pale, pane, pine, pins, pies

Activity 24
Answers will vary.
Possibilities include: eat, ear, lie, lice, lid, latch, iced, itch, ate, ache, ace, bare, bear, aid, beard, etched, tried, hare, car, cared, hid, cried, are, red, rid, bed, lit, lard

Activity 25
Answers will vary.

Activity 26
1. sport
2. math
3. van
4. pants
5. fan
6. bus
7. piano
8. ad
9. zoo
10. flu
11. exam
12. mic
13. o'clock
14. cinema
15. gym
16. wig

Activity 27
Answers will vary.

Activity 28
Answers will vary.

Activity 29
1. company
2. complex
3. computer
4. comments, compass
5. companion, comparison, communication
6. combined, command, complicated
7. committee, complete, compare, communicate

a. combined
b. command
c. comments
d. committee
e. communicate
f. communication
g. companion
h. company
i. compare
j. comparison
k. compass
l. complete
m. complex
n. complicated
o. computer

Activity 30
1. known, frozen
2. chosen, began
3. worn, stolen
4. chosen, torn
5. rung, have
6. stolen, known
7. have, sung
8. driven, begun
9. began, chosen
10. fell, frozen
11. worn, rung
12. fallen, broken
13. sang, chosen
14. brought, stolen
15. rang, began

Activity 31
1. brunch
2. spork
3. moped
4. paratroops
5. smog
6. telethon
7. twirl
8. travelogue
9. glimmer
10. motel
11. motocross
12. splatter
13. Internet
14. flare
15. flurry
16. clash
17. slosh
18. e-mail
19. camcorder
20. hazmat

Activity 32
1. gargantuan
2. pertinent
3. fester
4. goad
5. culprit
6. quibble
7. C
8. A
9. F
10. E
11. D
12. B

Activity 33
1. a
2. d
3. d

Activity 34
1. d
2. c
3. a

Activity 35
1. d
2. b
3. b
4. d
5. b

Activity 36
1. 4 darts: 18, 18, 32, 32
2. 5 darts: 12, 12, 14, 14, 48
3. 6 darts: 12, 12, 12, 14, 18, 32

Activity 37
1. 19
2. 20
3. 42
4. 70
5. 12
6. 83

Activity 38
A. 2,313
B. 925
C. 1,082
D. 958
E. 1,369
F. 1,316
G. 1,370
H. 1,223
Total = 5,278

ANSWER KEY (cont.)

Activity 39
Clocks should show the
following times:
1. 9:30
2. 4:45
3. 3:30
4. 5:10
5. 3:47
6. 5:45

Activity 40
1. rectangular pyramid
2. triangular prism
3. pentagonal pyramid
4. hexagonal prism
5. triangular pyramid
   (tetrahedron)

Activity 41
1. 5 other ways (1. red,
   green, yellow; 2. green,
   red, yellow; 3. green,
   yellow, red; 4. yellow,
   red, green; 5. yellow,
   green, red)
2. 19 times (9, 19, 29, 39,
   49, 59, 69, 79, 89, 90,
   91, 92, 93, 94, 95, 96,
   97, 98, 99)
3. They're all squares of
   other numbers.

Activity 42
1. Similar: a, c, d
   Congruent: a, d
2. Similar: b, c, d
   Congruent: b, c
3. Similar: a, b, c, d
   Congruent: b, d
4. Similar: a, b, c
   Congruent: a, c
5. Similar: a, b, d
   Congruent: a, b
6. Similar: a, b
   Congruent: c, d

Activity 43
1. 4,843	7. 1,479
2. 1,479	8. 2,219
3. 4,873	9. 3,776
4. 2,556	10. 1,245
5. 1,245	11. 2,479
6. 4,873	12. 3,212

James Madison

Activity 44
1. 12	4. 195
2. 36	5. 22
3. 246 or 264	

Activity 45
Answers will vary.
Possibilities include:
2 + 4 + 5 + 7 and
1 + 3 + 6 + 8
1 + 4 + 5 + 8 and
2 + 3 + 6 + 7

Activity 46
1. decade	6. duet
2. tripod	7. pair
3. centipede	8. tricycle
4. six	9. five
5. octopus	

Activity 47
1. 24 1/2	7. 1,956
2. 95	8. 344
3. 37	9. 54 1/4
4. 135	10. 80
5. 29	11. 75
6. 182	12. 92

Activity 48

Activity 49
12 x 12 = 6 x 24
7 x 16 = 28 x 4
9 x 22 = 11 x 18
155 ÷ 5 = 20 + 11
184 ÷ 8 = 207 ÷ 9
378 + 540 = 27 x 34
3,865 − 2,996 = 423 + 446
13 x 15 = 5 x 39
398 + 447 = 924 − 79
62 x 7 = 1,346 − 912
634 − 237 = 1,153 − 756
54 x 23 = 138 x 9
14 x 41 = 3,444 ÷ 6

Activity 50
1. 40, 48	6. -8, -11
2. 125, 216	7. 9, 10.5
3. 81, 243	8. 7.33, 7.44
4. 13, 16	9. 31, 43
5. 8, 13	10. -7, -4

My, this is definitely a
hare-raising experience!

Activity 51
Answers will vary.

Activity 52

Start		30	164	148	128	105	135	117	156
141	151	148	100	112	5	71	97	53	134
164	29	123	114	129	89	158	121	101	147
155	67	106	122	43	109	111	165	7	126
47	139	9	150	113	116	142	104	179	152
3	115	143	130	2	163	99	41	73	102
107	98	159	96	88	127	84	179	120	140
103	144	96	13	163	37	80	229	199	161
59	124	13	163	38	80	160	132	167	110
137	92	131	138	81	160	132	87	157	94
11	157	17	90	154	86	125	119	173	133
145	118	91	166	85	146	77	85		Finish

Activity 53

1. 24: 4 (2 2), 6 (2 3)
2. 90: 6 (2 3), 15 (3 5)
3. 56: 4 (2 2), 14 (2 7)
4. 88: 4 (2 2), 22 (2 11)
5. 100: 10 (2 5), 10 (2 5)
6. 54: 6 (2 3), 9 (3 3)

ANSWER KEY (cont.)

Activity 54
Possible answers:

1.
2.
3.
4.
5.

Activity 55
Prepare a message to your friend using the alphabetical coordinate grid.

Activity 56
1. D, 222
2. E, 5
3. F, 9
4. C, 3,544
5. A, 88
6. B, 78
7. H, 3/4
8. G, 3
9. I, 12

Activity 57
Path B = 23

Activity 58
Across
2. 29.178
4. 7.64
6. 29.4
7. 21.9
9. 49
10. 0.84
12. 60
13. 4.14
14. 56.056
17. 33.544

Down
1. 1.88
2. 2.6402
3. 17.4
5. 8.44
6. 21.204
8. 12.8
11. 46.05
13. 4.86
15. 53.55
16. 0.34

Activity 59
(half a million) + (2 x 10^5) + (300,000) + (500,000 x 4) + (1/2 of 3,000,000) + (1 million minus 500,000) = 5,000,000

Activity 60
Red: 36
Blue: 41
Green: 13, 17, 19
Pink: 44
Yellow: 1
Brown: 40
Orange: 15
Purple: 46

Activity 61

	Start				Finish
1.52	$0.85 + \frac{9}{10}$	$\frac{17}{20} + \frac{3}{4}$	2.1	$2 - \frac{1}{8}$	$\frac{2}{1,000}$
$\frac{11}{12} + \frac{7}{12}$	$\frac{3}{4} + \frac{3}{4}$	1.85	$\frac{15}{16} + \frac{7}{8}$	$3 - 1\frac{7}{8}$	$\frac{10}{100} + \frac{100}{1,000}$
$\frac{7}{8} + \frac{7}{8}$	1.48	$\frac{9}{10} + \frac{1}{2}$	$\frac{38}{100} + \frac{7}{10}$	2.4 − 0.6	$1 - \frac{65}{100}$
1 − 0.45	$\frac{15}{16} + \frac{1}{2}$	$1 + \frac{25}{100}$	$\frac{11}{12} + \frac{5}{6}$	$\frac{8}{9} + \frac{1}{3}$	$\frac{3}{8} + \frac{1}{16}$
2 × 0.8	$\frac{17}{20} + 0.15$	$\frac{7}{8} + \frac{1}{2}$	$\frac{5}{8} + \frac{1}{4}$	$\frac{11}{12} - \frac{1}{4}$	0.74 − 0.19
$1\frac{3}{7} + \frac{1}{7}$	$\frac{95}{100} + \frac{3}{10}$	$1 - \frac{1}{20}$	110%	$\frac{13}{14}$	99%

Activity 62
He thought he would be a good drill sergeant.

Activity 63

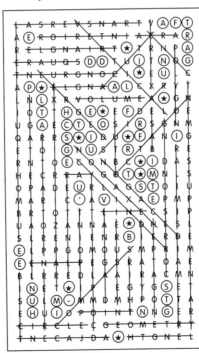

After adding up all the factors, I figure it must've been sum-thing.

Activity 64
Across
1. 10
2. 36
3. 80
4. 61
5. 15
6. 564
7. 500
8. 48
9. 40
10. 81
11. 217
12. 19
13. 2,500
15. 9,000
16. 192
17. 20
18. 160
19. 12
20. 5,921
23. 622
25. 27

Down
1. 10
2. 344
3. $8.10
4. 67
5. $12.30
6. 50
7. 561
8. 472
9. 400
10. 89
11. 212
12. 10
14. 570
15. 901
16. 10
17. 211
18. 122
20. 250
22. 200
23. 60
24. 223

Activity 65
1. 7/1,000, .7%
2. .667, 66.7%
3. 3/4, 75%
4. 3/50, .06
5. 1/2, .5
6. 5/9, 55.5%
7. .04, 4%
8. 19/50, 38%
9. 7/9, 77.7%
10. .9375, 93.75%
11. 11/25, .44
A lot of hoop-la and fan-fare!

Activity 66
1. 13,589 or 15,789
2. 864,210
3. 98,791
4. 1,805,077

Activity 67

1. S	10. N
2. H	11. G
3. E	12. O
4. W	13. M
5. A	14. K
6. T	15. U
7. R	16. P
8. Y	17. D
9. I	

She was trying to make up her mind.

Activity 68

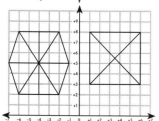

Activity 69

Across

1. 339,933	17. 7,117
5. 525	19. 868
7. 37,573	21. 4,334
9. 6,666	22. 515
10. 2,552	23. 78,587
11. 77	24. 72,327
13. 33	26. 454
15. 40,304	27. 12,721

Down

1. 37,673	14. 373
2. 9,669	15. 414
3. 33	16. 48,184
4. 37,273	18. 13,631
5. 575	20. 65,756
6. 232	21. 4,774
8. 55	22. 55
11. 707	23. 777
12. 888	25. 22

Activity 70

1. 30	6. 72
2. 13.5	7. 21
3. 78	8. 31
4. 15	9. 1.5
5. 1	10. 20.7

Will E. Everdrop

Activity 71

1. fat / plump
2. shed / barn
3. boat / ship
4. bare / bald
5. nap / slumber
6. hop / leap
7. bead / pearl
8. scram / escape
9. talk / speak
10. piece / part

Activity 72

Answers may vary.
Possibilities include:
1. dentist
2. veterinarian
3. singer
4. actor
5. website designer
6. firefighter
7. teacher
8. photographer
9. seamstress/tailor
10. pilot
11. realtor
12. runner/athlete

Activity 73

Objects in the box: horn, chair, cap, pencil, dog, glass, key, bell, fork, sandwich, apple, book, whistle, spoon, backpack, paddle, bicycle, cup, jump rope

Activity 74

1. foot
2. heart
3. hands
4. back
5. skin, teeth
6. lip
7. eye, eye
8. throat
9. limb
10. head, shoulders
11. neck
12. belly
13. wrist
14. ear
15. skin, bones

Activity 75

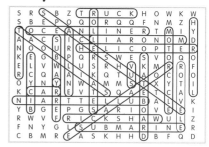

1. airplane
2. bicycle
3. bullet train
4. car
5. elevator
6. escalator
7. ferry
8. helicopter
9. hydrofoil
10. monorail
11. motorcycle
12. ocean liner
13. rickshaw
14. roller skates
15. sailboat
16. skateboard
17. space shuttle
18. submarine
19. subway
20. SUV
21. tanker
22. truck

Activity 76

Directions to BC Place Stadium will vary.

ANSWER KEY (cont.)

Activity 77

Across

3.	world	11.	air
5.	up	12.	cherries
7.	bug	14.	oats
8.	nine	16.	heels
9.	apple		

Down

1.	dollars	7.	beans
2.	down	10.	milk
4.	dumps	13.	heaven
6.	heart	15.	arm

Activity 78

1.

2.

Activity 79

1. FSERVEDOURTERMS
2. FSERVEDOURERMST
3. FSERVEDOURERMLT
4. FSERVEDOUROOERMLT
5. FRSEVEDOUROOERMLT
6. FREVEDOUROOSERMLT
7. FREVKDOUROOSERMLT
8. FRMVKDOUROOSERELT
9. FRMVKDOUROOSEELT
10. FRMKDOUROOSEVELT
11. FRMKDROOSEVELT
12. FRANMKDROOSEVELT
13. FRANKMDROOSEVELT
14. FRANKLDROOSEVELT
15. FRANKLINDROOSEVELT

Activity 80

1.	bee	7.	ball
2.	grand	8.	clip
3.	thumb	9.	fly
4.	hand	10.	go
5.	fan	11.	you
6.	bread	12.	word

Activity 81

Answers will vary.

Activity 82

1.	Russ	5.	Ryan
2.	Andrew	6.	Danny
3.	Jeff	7.	Alan
4.	Zac	8.	Mark

Activity 83

1. North (or South) Carolina
2. Honolulu
3. Jefferson City
4. Indiana (or Indianapolis)
5. Texas
6. St. Paul
7. Kentucky
8. Hartford
9. Helena
10. Jackson
11. Richmond
12. Idaho
13. Trenton
14. Frankfort
15. California
16. Juneau
17. Louisiana
18. Maryland
19. Delaware
20. Charleston
21. Kentucky
22. Annapolis

Activity 84

1. goat, eel, slug
2. gerbil, boar, lobster, zebra
3. tuna, trout, panda, loon
4. llama, ostrich, cat
5. mouse, cardinal, skunk
6. robin, monkey, tuna, cow
7. horse, rat, wasp, deer

Activity 84

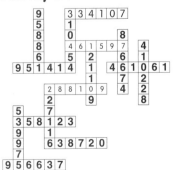

Activity 86

1.	lime, mile
2.	pace, cape
3.	deal, lead
4.	loot, tool
5.	cane, acne
6.	bard, drab
7.	live, vile
8.	fits, fist
9.	melons, lemons
10.	life, file
11.	pore, rope

Activity 87

1. tricycle
2. Quit following me!
3. pie in the face
4. age before beauty
5. circles under the eyes
6. double date
7. long time no see
8. split decision
9. one in a million
10. go for it
11. slow down
12. stand in the corner

Activity 88

1.	first	8.	star
2.	alone	9.	Richmond
3.	wool	10.	toy
4.	dark	11.	gulp
5.	feast	12.	grammar
6.	bottom	13.	hat
7.	door	14.	mat

food for thought

Activity 89

1.	meat	9.	lamb, sheep
2.	fawn	10.	horse
3.	yellow	11.	glass slipper
4.	dog	12.	blue and yellow
5.	William	13.	acorn
6.	golf	14.	niece
7.	lion	15.	top
8.	ten		

Activity 90

1.
B	F	D
C	A	E
I	H	G

2.
E	H	C
B	A	G
F	D	I

3.
F	B	E
G	C	D
A	H	I

Activity 91

1. reynard, vixen, kit
2. doe, kid, herd
3. bull, calf, pod
4. lion, lion, pride
5. kangaroo, buck, mob
6. ewe, lamb, flock
7. bull, cow, calf
8. bull, pup, pod
9. pig, boar, sow
10. rooster, hen, hatchling
11. chicken, rooster, chick
12. goose, gander, gosling

Activity 92

1. D
2. B
3. H
4. V
5. Y
6. O
7. A
8. M
9. G
10. L
11. E
12. R
13. T
14. I
15. Patrick Henry

"Give me liberty or give me death."

Activity 93

1. Betty, 6:15, spaghetti
2. Charlie, 6:00, rolls
3. Heidi, 6:30, salad
4. Paul, 5:45, dessert
5. Roland, 6:45, soda

Activity 94

1. Atlantic Ocean
2. equator
3. Tasman Sea
4. Ural Mountains
5. Indian Ocean
6. Central America
7. prime meridian
8. Indian Ocean
9. Mediterranean Sea
10. Pacific Ocean
11. Atlantic Ocean
12. equator
13. Red Sea/Indian Ocean
14. Drake Passage
15. Pacific Ocean

Activity 95

1. Ralph, pie
2. Mary, stuffing
3. Johnny, potatoes
4. Susie, bread rolls
5. Bill, corn
6. Ann, green beans
7. Jeffrey, turkey
8. Angie, ham

Activity 96

1. Giants
2. Warriors
3. Saints
4. Cowboys
5. Yankees
6. Kings
7. Suns
8. Heat
9. Bulls
10. Wild
11. Rangers
12. Twins
13. Cubs
14. Colts
15. Jets
16. Rams
17. Browns
18. Rockets
19. Clippers
20. Hornets

Activity 97

"I do solemnly swear that I will faithfully execute the office of President of the United States, and will to the best of my ability, preserve, protect, and defend the Constitution of the United States."

Activity 98

1. soldier
2. vaccine
3. Braille
4. Dodgers
5. aviator
6. skating
7. peanuts
8. authors
9. dancing
10. senator
11. chemist

Activity 99

Stickers are divided as follows:

Lyndsay = 1 dog, 1, balloon, 3 cat

Juliana = 1 dog, 1 balloon, 1 planet, 2 owl

Jon = 2 dog, 1 cat, 1 planet, 1 owl

Steve = 1 dog, 1 balloon, 2 planet, 1 owl

Morgan = 2 balloon, 1 cat, 1 planet, 1 owl

Activity 100

Possible paths:

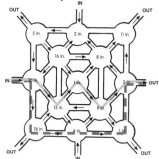

Activity 101

1. jazz
2. quiet
3. yucky
4. x-ray
5. violin
6. bashful
7. wrong or grown
8. defeat
9. koala
10. molar
11. porcupine
12. profit
13. balcony
14. defend
15. require
16. mysterious
17. laughter
18. jacket
19. exactly
20. vowel
21. consonant
22. zebra